We Dwell in Possibilities

What American Women Think about Practically Everything!

by

Carlotta G. Holton

The contents of this work, including, but not limited to, the accuracy of events, people, and places depicted; opinions expressed; permission to use previously published materials included; and any advice given or actions advocated are solely the responsibility of the author, who assumes all liability for said work and indemnifies the publisher against any claims stemming from publication of the work.

All Rights Reserved
Copyright © 2019 by Carlotta G. Holton

No part of this book may be reproduced or transmitted, downloaded, distributed, reverse engineered, or stored in or introduced into any information storage and retrieval system, in any form or by any means, including photocopying and recording, whether electronic or mechanical, now known or hereinafter invented without permission in writing from the publisher.

ISBN: 978-1-4809-9158-3
eISBN: 978-1-4809-9372-3

Contents

Introduction v
Demographics ... Who We Are xi
The Story Behind the Story xv
Careers 1
Occupational Rewards 5
Occupational Drawbacks 9
Misperceptions about Jobs 15
Not Just One Career Anymore, Multi-tasking Successfully 19
Career Advice 23
Gender Parity: Fair Play? 29
Relationships: How Do They Rate? 33
Relationships: What Could Be Improved? .37
Children and Parenting 41
Religious or Spiritual 45
Morality: A Bankrupt Commodity? 51
The State of the Union: Comfort Level with the Country's Economy 55
Life Now Better, Worse, or Same as Growing Up 61
Good Health is Priceless 65
Concerns/Solutions for Yourself and Aging Family Members 69
Fight or Flight? 75
Home Ownership 79
Hobbies 81
Staying Social 87
Travel 91
Reading 95
What's for Dinner? 99

To Market, to Market	101
Watching TV	105
Pets	109
Location – Location – Location	113
Biggest Fear	119
Disappointments	123
Dreaming Big	127
Parents' Impact on You	131
Sports	137
Culture	141
America: One Language for All?	145
Retirement	151
Final Decisions	155
Gun Control	157
Life and This Stage	163
Conclusions	169
Questionnaire	173
Sources	179
Acknowledgments	181
Other Books by Carlotta G. Holton	183

Introduction

"Women are the real architects of society."
~ *Harriet Beecher Stowe*

As women, we are constantly evolving. Changing attitudes toward our gender have accommodated many, but not all. Still, we are told, it is progress. A fair number of females can enter a career path never before considered and, for the most part, be accepted. Females can choose not to marry, not to have children, or become a single parent. There is far less rebuke for such choices by society than previously. The sting of such stigma is far less painful or shameful.

We can marry someone of the same sex, younger or older, regardless of race, ethnicity, or religion. The lines, for the most part, between sexism, ageism, and racism have blurred, though are still visible.

So, if as we were told years ago in the 1968 Virginia Slims cigarette commercial, "We've come a long way baby," just where do we stand now? Do we still adhere to Helen Reddy's unofficial 1971 anthem of the women's movement, "I am Woman"? It depends on who you ask and where you do the asking.

The Roper Organization of *Fortune Magazine* posed this issue examining the years from 1932 to the 1950s from the perspective of social and cultural angles. The conclusion? While few men favored women in the marketplace in the 30s, by 1946, 70 percent agreed men and women doing the same job should receive equal pay. While this same survey found that 25 percent explained their rationale for saying women doing certain jobs did not match those of men, by 1993, only 13 percent frowned upon the equal pay for equal work mantra.

Evolution is often slow. We must ask ourselves, are we still mired in the same gender-stereotyped career? Have we stood toe to toe with men in career opportunities and promotions?

Have we learned to adapt to more than one career choice? Are we flexible enough to work and be a mother effectively? Are we more prone to everyday prayer and organized religion, or do we label ourselves as "spiritual" instead?

Have we become world-wide travelers or never left home? Are we up on the world's state of affairs and how it affects us here? How frequently do we pursue cultural activities, like the theater, movies, museums, concerts? Are we involved within our cities and communities, or do we suffer from "not enough time"? Are we where we want to be right now? If not, when is it likely to happen?

How confident are we about the country we live in? How do we perceive the future for ourselves and our children, families, and generations to come? Are we bogged down with the perceptions of our generational titles – Gen X, Millennials, Baby Boomers? Can we get beyond such labels and stretch our imaginations and creativity?

In this age of technology, do we still read books, newspapers, or magazines? Have we joined a book club to expand our horizons and expose ourselves to the choices of others? Do we spend hours upon end watching television, only watch select programs or specials, or have we forsaken the television completely? Have the laptop computer, iPod, and cellphone become the new technological umbilical cords which we cannot effectively sever?

Reality in many cases slaps us in the face. The global perspective for world peace isn't pretty.

Fears of Russia have resurrected, and the prospect of nuclear disaster looms from North Korea. Few would contest the notion that the world is a frightening place. Headlines scream about conflict in the Middle East: *Hezzbolah Vows to Slaughter Saudi Forces*, if they try to invade Iraq. Some proclaimed Americans have fought with, joined, and stand accused of providing material or financial support to extremist groups like ISIS. We are cautioned to report any suitcase or boxes left abandoned in public spaces, for it could be a bomb, part of a terrorist attack in the US. *Washington Post* news polls support the notion that a majority of us believe that the country is at war with "radical Islam."

A Feb. 7, 2017, Quinnipiac University Poll asserts that 70 percent of voters say they believe a terrorist attack in the USA resulting in large causalities is "very" likely in the near future.

Our global world has grown smaller. The Zika virus reared its ugly head for the first time in early 2015 in Brazil. There have now been cases in America. This past fall, doctors noticed a spike in the number of babies with a serious congenital brain deformity call microcephaly – when an infant is born with an underdeveloped brain and skull.

It seems our daily lives are always being challenged. And then there are scams via telephone in which allegedly the IRS is calling to inform you they are suing you for back taxes. They instruct you stay on cell phone, go to the bank and withdraw a certain amount, and redeposit it into another bank. All the while threatening if you don't, the sheriff will be at your door to arrest you and confiscate your home and all of your belongings.

The 2012 job market was dire as well, with 60 percent of US college graduates unable to find a full-time job in their chosen profession, according to job placement firm Adecco. The term, "Generation Jobless," was aptly coined with college grads under 24 facing an uncertain job future. Compounding their quest is the exorbitant cost of tuition. Along with that coveted sheepskin comes a decade's long debt to be paid when they begin work, if they can find a job commensurate with the time and money they have invested in their education.

Are things improving? According to the Economic Policy Institute, the class of 2017 has much brighter prospects. Of course, it all depends on where the jobs are located. The fact that more US companies have bailed out of the United States because of taxes and moved to Mexico, Canada, and China contributes to the problem of unemployment. Many express hope that with his business acumen, a reversal will take place with the election of President Donald J. Trump.

As a journalist, I am curious how the everyday woman feels about her life amidst this brave new world. We know how Hollywood celebrities feel, but what about the woman who runs a combine on a farm in northern Missouri? Or the woman in Montana who deals with bias working on a Native American reservation? How do these issues impact the woman who works three jobs to support her family? What about the woman who is caring for her aging parents? What is the feeling of a young California single mother of six who is barely able to support her children?

How do the events in the world and in this country affect their lives at present? What part do they have in shaping the future of the generations to come? Do their opinions really matter? Do these women who come from all 50 states share a common belief in the morality of the nation?

Or do educational level, religious belief, paychecks, and geography channel their notions into a helter/skelter type of thinking? Do women come together on the issues that face our nation, or are they miles apart?

Immigration issues are a hotbed topic for all of us. There are over 300 cities, counties, and states that are considered "sanctuary cities." These jurisdictions protect criminal aliens from deportation by refusing to comply with Immigration and Customs Enforcement (ICE) detainers or otherwise impede open communication and information exchanges between their employees or offices and federal immigration agents. And many times in communities across the country, agitated citizen's crowd into town hall meetings to try to prevent detention facilities from coming in their backyards.

Health concerns abound in this country. Do we favor the use of medical marijuana farms? How satisfied/dissatisfied are we with our current school programs in both rural, suburban, and urban milieus? Younger Baby Boomers and Millennials worry about Medicare and Medicaid, and the list goes on.

I have thought long and hard about these issues which face all women. The result was a survey aimed at reaching as many women in this country as possible. I did not seek women representing one religion, job or career, socioeconomic strata, or race. I purposely avoided any political questions, though invariably some answers touched upon government administration at its highest level. Does their economic status put a crimp on their attending movies, concerts, museums, and theater? I wanted to know their fears and disappointments. Many of us find ourselves examining some of the issues our ancestors faced when emigrating to America decades ago. In a land filled with a myriad of cultures, should the country speak more than one language, or is English, the only "official" one, to be taught? Should equal opportunities for advanced education, driver's licenses, and medical care apply to undocumented immigrants?

The violent and bloody carnages witnessed in schools and streets throughout the country have scarred us. Depending on what part of the country is your home, these horrific acts have further cemented our views on the prospect of gun control. But how do you ban hunting in rural areas, where game is literally the diet of a family? Conversely, what do you say to an inner-city woman whose child has been shot through an open window while she is studying her lessons? Like America itself, the answers are not clear.

I did not inquire salaries but merely asked about their satisfaction in terms of adequate recompense for their jobs. I want to know what women really think about their occupations and how they would advise other young women entering the field. How prepared or unprepared are they for a sudden career change forced on them by a struggling economy?

The women participating in the survey ranged 20 to 94. On the younger end of the spectrum, I wanted young women to have graduated high school or the equivalent and have been working or furthering their education for a two-year period. This was the only caveat to participation. No political affiliations, religious beliefs, marital status, race, or income levels were asked. In fact, I sought as great a divergence in these areas as possible. I was out to prove that no matter where we lived, where we worked, if we even worked outside the home, what our child rearing attitudes were, and how comfortable we are in this society, we are still very much THE SAME. We all *need* the same things to lead happy, healthy and productive lives.

From the Black Hills of South Dakota to the panhandle of Florida, from an island in Maine to horse ranches deep in the heart of Texas, from the bright lights of New York's Broadway to the vineyards of California, women strongly asserted their opinions. Along with their family's favorite dishes they cook, these women offered some intriguing food for thought.

(See if you agree or disagree with the participants by taking the survey at the end of the book.)

Demographics

"A woman is like a tea bag - you can't tell how strong she is until you put her in hot water."
                                        ~ *Eleanor Roosevelt*

The sample includes 162 women ages 20 to 94. Women represented all 50 of the United States. The good news is that 100 percent hold high school or GED diplomas. The survey, conducted January 2013 through November 2017, indicated that 35 percent attended high school only; 13.1 percent completed two year-business degree/certification programs, junior college, trade school or secretarial-type training; 37.5 percent had college degrees, 11.2 percent attained Master's degrees while 3 percent held a PHD, MD or Vet MD.

Of the participants, 49.3 percent are married, 11.3 percent single, 4.4 percent in a long-term, committed relationship, 15.1 percent were divorced, 12 percent widowed, 6.3 divorced and remarried. Women with children accounted for 75 percent of the survey, while those who did not have children made up the remaining 25 percent.

Occupations Represented
Accountant
Adjunct instructor
Administrative assistant
Advertising
Air force senior airman (E-4)

Airline personnel
Architectural designer
Art gallery owner
Artist
Attorney
Author
Bartender
Beauty salon owner
Calendar administrator in law firm
Casino cashier
Catalogue customer service
Chef
Chemist
Chiropractor
College professor
Claims adjustor
College student
Commercial bank lender
Commercial insurance manager
Commercial real estate paralegal
Cook
Cleaning service entrepreneur
Computer programmer
Convenience store cashier
Crisis support manager
Customer phone sales
Dance teacher and owner of studio
Director of Marketing/public relations for major zoo
Disability service sports manager
Dog groomer
Dog trainer
Doula
Dude ranch owner
Editor
Elementary school teacher
Engineer

Environmental Education School Programs Specialist, Roger Williams Zoo
Farm animal consultant
Florist
Front desk clerk at a hotel/restaurant
Graphic Designer
Hairdresser
Homemaker
Horse trainer
Human resources
Insurance adjustor
Interior designer
IT project manager
Law enforcement
Lay ministry
Legislative liaison
Librarian
Licensed practical nurse
Limousine driver
Loan documentation specialist
Manager of Ambassador Animal Programming, Roger Williams Zoo
Massage therapist
Medical coder
Medical technologist/research associate
Mental health therapist
Model
Musical theater performer
Mortuary beautician
Music teacher
Native American Indian educator
Nanny
N.J. Transit bus driver
Part-time photo journalist
Part-time realtor
Parochial school elementary school teacher
Performing ministry
Payroll clerk

Pediatrician
Personal care attendant
Pharmacist
Pharmacy owner
Print shop worker
Property manager
PSI/PSI project coordinator (Responsible for coordinating and scheduling installations by reviewing and managing Installed Sales paperwork and contacting installers)
Psychiatric nurse
Public relations coordinator
Radiologist
Rehab counselor for the deaf
Registered nurse in operating room
Sales
Scene painter
School bus driver
Seamstress at a blouse factory
Seamstress at bridal shop
Special education teacher
Swimming instructor
Senior citizen housing coordinator
Speech pathologist
Standardized patient acting coach for doctors
Thrift shop proprietor
Travel agent
TV producer
US Postal worker
Veterinarian
Video sales
Waitress
Wedding chapel manager
Wedding and events planner
Wedding design/decorating business
Work exploration coordinator for people with disabilities
Writer

The Story Behind the Story

Many of the women I have approached have labeled this an overwhelming project. Their questions were valid ones. *How will you find the women? How will you entice them to participate with truly honest answers?* (Sometimes honesty requires anonymity, they suggested.) *How can you determine which questions will best monitor the pulse of women's current issues and future concerns? What response options will you provide? With such a daunting task how long do you think it will take? What do you hope to prove?*

My initial task was to formulate a questionnaire. This part was easy since I consider myself to be current with the topics of the day. I am an educated, experienced writer and educator who has been married, widowed, and remarried, and the mother of an adult son. I actually had to edit the number of questions and still had a few women respond with, "whew!" when they were done with the four-page survey. Yet the questions were stimulating as indicated by the responses and triggered in many deep feelings of love, joy, angst, fear, and hope. More than one woman thanked me for the opportunity to review her perspective and revise her goals. While not pointedly asked, women also subtly and overtly voiced opinions on politics, world leaders, financial concerns, gender relationships, and past experiences for which they would like a "do over."

Where did I find these women? I cultivated some from my friends, acquaintances, and professional colleagues I know from numerous states around the country. In turn, I asked them to ask friends, colleagues or neighbors for their assistance. From here I turned to relatives in the Midwest and south east, asking them also to "pass it on." I used my resources from press contacts through writer associations to which I have belonged and from there tried various women's community organizations, such as Junior League chapters, book clubs, La Leche groups, and Ys. Finally, I approached state travel bureaus, libraries, and various clubs for sailing, riding, and skiing.

I met with women who are avid knitters, quilters, and those who shoot at gun ranges. I even contacted state historic parks and zoos to identify women who would find this an interesting project.

I wanted to have as many vocations as possible represented. I didn't want all teachers and nurses but looked to physicians and pharmacists and veterinarians. I also sought out women who toiled as farmers, cleaned septic tanks, styled the hair for the deceased in mortuaries, worked in casinos, and drove limousines for a living. I was not seeking to get the opinions of merely college-educated women, but a broad-based group of women who represented a healthy portion of the entire country.

Many women felt comfortable knowing I would not be using last names in the survey, though I do have that information. A couple who had more unusual first names requested they use their middle names instead. This anonymity opened the flood gates of emotions that women expressed when it came to difficult jobs, failing relationships, and fervent hopes and dreams. I am so grateful for this candor, and I am convinced it's what makes this book so very special and meaningful for all women.

I offered choices when it came to filing their applications. Some women requested to receive the questionnaire via email and responded in like fashion. A few wanted a hard copy mailed to their home addresses with an included self-addressed stamped envelope. Another popular response was to conduct telephone interviews. I offered these three avenues for them to choose their preference in their response. On a book tour out to the Midwest and western states, I conducted interviews face to face with women that I encountered. Out of the many women who I invited to participate, I can count on two hands the number of women who declined the opportunity to be heard.

As to the question how long it would take, I had no immediate answer. I knew I wanted to reach representation from each of the 50 states, and I wanted at least 100 women. That, as I correctly anticipated, might take longer than I would have liked. After my efforts, research, writing, and editing it has taken nearly four years to complete the project. I have met some wonderful women who have shown me that no matter where we live, what we do for a living, our marital status, children/no children, economic status, race, religion and non-believers, we all have very much in common when it comes to our life's hopes and outlook for the future.

As I noted, this project has taken four years to complete, and as I see, it is an ongoing slice of our lives. During this time, political administrations have changed from Democratic President Barack Obama to Republican President Donald Trump. Within the pages of this book, there will be reference to both, depending on the dates the forms were completed. During this time frame, we have witnessed many political tensions from abroad and within the country from special interest groups, political rivals, and terrorists. Some of these have been addressed, others not, as it depended on the time frame the questioner was responding.

I admire all of the women who participated in this survey. In their own way, each are intelligent, strong, caring, and remarkable women. As to their final question, "What do you hope to prove?"

I will let the reader be the judge. What do you think?

Careers

"People think that at the end of the day that a man is the only answer (to fulfillment). Actually a job is better for me."
~ Princess Diana

One of the participants in the survey objected to my use of the word "career." When I checked the various dictionaries, I found that the following words, "vocation, job, occupation, profession, calling, livelihood, and line of business" were all synonyms for the word career.

For some women, their career was a calling. Something about a vocation internally spoke to them to investigate and explore this job. Others were led there by references or monetary concerns regarding the ability to pay for college or training school classes.

Back in the 50s and 60s, it was commonly accepted that upon high school graduation, women would enter one of three areas of advancement, depending on intelligence and affordability to further their education. Nursing, teaching, and secretarial work were on one list, while beautician, dental assistant, and business careers were backup positions.

Options were often further limited by the myths perpetuated by men and society. The message seemed to be that if you are ambitious, you will be punished. If you focus on your career, no man will have you. Even if you do marry, you'll never have children. And if by some miracle you do manage to have kids, you are going to ruin them. In every case, you will end your days regretting your choices.

The stereotypes have changed, somewhat. They now stretch to include a woman's marital status, her mental status, and eventual success. Women who postponed marriage, for example, would end up old, crazy, and alone. Yet the famous 1986 assertion – that a woman who hits 40 without marrying has a better chance of being killed by a terrorist than of having a wedding – proved so decisively wrong that even its chief perpetrator (*Newsweek*) in a story titled, "The Marriage Crunch," dated June 6, 2006, took it all back 20 years later.

By 2010, the 30-to-40-year-olds who worried about never having a white dress or eating over-frosted cake were 53 to 63 years old – 23 years older than they were when that article ran. And according to the US Census, only 7 percent of women in that age group never married. What really happened is that the increasing number of older singles entering the workforce in the 70s happened to coincide with a sharp increase in the marriage age. We married late, but we did get married.

Another myth that was perpetuated was that even if you do get married, you'll die childless. (There was no other assumption than that **ALL** women **should** and **would** have children.) Sometime in the last 30 years, the words "biological clock" came to be associated with the looming risk of childlessness.

Another popular stereotype banned women from entering the sciences. *Women in the survey are not those women.* Not only have they successfully traversed into other fields, but many entered second or third careers or established businesses of their own. And women are backing up their resumes with skills than can adapt to changes in the future. We are truly not a one career nation any longer. In fact, many of the women in the survey noted they have had more than one occupation/career to date.

Stephanie from Hilo, UT, has worked as a bartender, waitress, and had an office job. "Now, I am a stay-at-home mom." She thinks all of her jobs have made her the person she is today, having learned different skills.

In some cases, the job chose the women. Elizabeth from WV, a communications officer said, "The job chose me. Originally, I was in human resources directed by a community technology college. The position grew, and I grew with it."

As a single mom, one octogenarian noted that her job as a secretary to a manager also expanded. "I helped in any way I could. As a new program started, I would adapt and was appreciative of the increase in title and pay, as I needed to support my child."

For Sheila of Tannersville, PA, "My life in retail was difficult. I chose the career because I love to interact with people and find them very interesting. But there is no life outside. You work weekends and holidays, and that's tough if you are raising a family."

For 40 years Elaine from Ashville, AL, worked as a newspaper reporter, a magazine features writer, newspaper editor, and by the time her second child came along, "I found it easier to work from home than an outside office. It was great because I set my own schedule, mindful of deadlines."

Diane of South Kingstown, RI, said, "I fell into my career in public relations and marketing." Diane, who is employed at the Roger Williams Park and Zoo, explained, "I liked to write and work with media – it just made sense. Moreover, nothing stays the same, so it was and still is exciting.

"There is always something new to market, a different medium to use to present an organization's mission."

Nannette of Surprise, AZ, feels she was "born to work in the disability field." A disability service manager in the sports industry, she explained, "My father is a minister, and my mom is a nurse. I remember going to nursing homes as a small child and being trained in CPR and respite care as a teenager. I'm not passionate about my field because it's my job; I got this job because I am passionate about what I do."

Phyllis of Fountain Valley, CA, has been a teacher for 20 years. "I knew when I was in grade school I wanted to be a teacher. This career picked me."

Gail of Magnolia, DE, also said, "I didn't choose it; I fell into it." The property insurance examiner started in a clerical position and someone "saw a potential in me and asked me if I wanted to be an adjuster trainee, and I jumped on the opportunity."

Jeanine's entrée into real estate was a more unusual means. The Honolulu, HI, resident said, "We had vacant, undeveloped property, and I thought why give it away, when I can make some money on it? So, I entered real estate and got to meet people, checked out lots of homes and got good commissions."

Practical issues of life is what prompted Lisa from Indianapolis, IN, to enter the world of banking. "I got into this field originally to pay the rent."

Jasmine's "passion for nature and the environment" led her into her career in environmental education as a school programs specialist at the Roger Williams Zoo in RI. The Dartmouth, MA, resident said, "I wanted to share and inspire others to care too and make better green choices in their lives. To raise the next generation of environmental stewards."

Tania of Annapolis, MD, found her way into chiropractic at the young age of 15. "I found the field as I was searching for college scholarship money. I've worked in this field for 25 years and it has been a wonderfully rewarding career in every way."

For many of the women who participated in the survey, children were the motivation for their choices. Thelma from Great Falls, MT, was initially a hair dresser but became an Indian Education Coordinator for 21 years. "I loved working with Native American children and their families. It's as simple as that."

Nursing was an accidental choice for Randolph, NJ, resident Roberta. "I did not get accepted to Georgetown for International Relations/Language studies. Nursing was my backup plan. Plus, I spent six months as a helper in a French hospital and fell in love with the art of surgery."

Sometimes fate has a way of taking charge of our lives. Such was the case with Eileen of Las Vegas, NV, who is the assistant manager at a wedding chapel. "The field chose me. I got a limousine license and became a driver and found it was such great fun. This led to me discovering the wedding chapel business which I love. We do all kind of themed weddings such as Star Wars. So it's always different and never boring. I meet people from all over the country as well."

"The excitement of travel for myself and my family is what drew me into careers as a customer service agent for two major airlines and hotels," said Thelma from Cary, NC.

Parental influence was the major reason Gloria, Wilmington, VT, chose teaching as a career. "Back then women had fewer options than the usual, secretary, teacher or nurse."

Jennifer of Scituate, RI, said she chose her career as the manager of Ambassador Animal Programming at the Roger Williams Zoo, "because I wanted to work with animals. I really love people, too. Behavior change fascinates me. I am passionate about the environment and conservation. My career allows me to do all of it!"

Occupational Rewards

"The most difficult thing is the decision to act, the rest is merely tenacity. The fears are paper tigers. You can do anything you decide to do. You can act to change and control your life; and the procedure, the process is its own reward."
~ Amelia Earhart

The term "rewards" when defining the benefits of a career are truly something that differs from one vocation to the next. One woman's reward may be a nuisance for another in the same or different field. This in itself is why we should celebrate the uniqueness and talents of every woman. Each in their own way, makes meaningful contributions to our society and future generations. In addition, what makes someone have feelings of elation for a job well done also varies amongst individuals.

For example, graphic designers appreciate the fact that they get to share their work online, which is viewed on social media channels and platforms like *Pinterest*. This opens up an endless stream of opportunities and can lead to making great working contacts in the industry. Another advantage is that it can be done from home. This also means you can pretty much set your own hours.

For other women, enjoying a job is reward in itself. Eileen, a manager of a Las Vegas wedding chapel says, "It's a lot fun. Especially the themed weddings. I've seen Star Wars characters, Disney characters, and many other scenarios incorporated into the ceremonies. You don't leave here depressed."

Helping others is at the heart of many of those who enter the medical field. Anita of OK, has been a personal care attendant for the past 15 years. "I enjoy improving someone's life. It's also never boring as every day is something new."

Nancy, a retired corporate attorney, explained, "After graduating from college I took a course to become a paralegal. I found the work interesting so went on to law school. A law degree can open up lots of opportunities. One can set up a practice, but there are also jobs in government and the business world."

Some of the women loved animals and the environment and were successfully able to combine these interests into a career. Jennifer of Scituate, RI, said, "The Roger William Zoo offers flex time in my department. I am able to work full time and (usually) spend a lot of time with my young children."

Bri of Columbia, MD, is a college graduate working in video sales for a major company selling DVD's through the mail and online. "The scheduling allows me to finish my schooling," she said.

Pam of Indianapolis works as a commercial real estate paralegal.

Tatiana of Rhode Island enjoys her job working for Verizon. "I enjoy helping people and it gives me a good feeling."

Heather from Portland, OR, loves the challenge of nursing in the northwest. Originally from PA, she said, "I enjoy the travel and meeting new people and living in another part of the country, though I do miss my family."

Nancy from Surprise, AZ, works as a financial advisor for a major firm. "I'm lucky because I am able to work from home."

Linda of Langhorne, PA, drives a NJ Transit bus. She described her fulfillment in helping people with an example. "One time I had an empty bus on the start of my run. As I was heading out on my route, I saw a five car pile-up on the highway. Glass was flying everywhere. I was proud to be the first person to call in for help. Those times are really special knowing I helped someone in need."

Humanitarian rewards aside, many women said they yearned for a job that offered fulfillment for them personally. They sought out positions which not only were beneficial to others, but also that capitalized on using their intelligence to the maximum. These women said they enjoyed testing their skills.

Pamela of Randolph, NJ, is a pharmacist. "I chose the career to help people and to be part of a respected profession and to have a job at which my mind is challenged."

Jasmine of Dartmouth, MA, said the advantage of her position with the Roger Williams Zoo is that "I get a sense of making a difference. There is a satisfaction of getting through to a student, witnessing them have a 'Wow' moment when something clicks. Working with animals! Variety that every day is different and so rewarding."

Diane of Kingstown, RI, said, "Nonprofit marketing/public relations gives me the opportunity to promote and organization or an idea that could make a difference in an individual's life. Also, the field is transportable. I can go anywhere and find work."

Elaine of Ashville, AL, said, "My job allows me to work from home and set my own schedules."

Diane of Anchorage, AK, is a writer and editor doing engineering studies. "I can work independently, set my own pace within reason and work collaboratively with others. The job offers good pay with the right government agency or private corporations."

Disability service manager Nannette of Surprise, AZ, said, "I get to make sure people with disabilities enjoy sporting events like concerts. I also enjoy occasionally sharing tickets with family and friends."

"For me, being an administrative assistant is easy," said Elizabeth of Westbrook, CT. "I'm able to feel a sense of accomplishment and like being part of a team."

Those in the banking field shared the pluses of their positions.

Linda of Plainfield, IL said, "We get great holidays and I don't work nights or weekends."

Linda of Indianapolis, IN, agrees. "Banking is a reliable source of income and you learn the aspects of banking. It also helps me in other financial areas of my personal life. Things that most people would not normally understand, I now have a better insight into – specifically finances."

University assistant professor Lydia of Newark, DE, said, "The advantages include more time with my family. The schedule is flexible for me to make a real and lasting impression on college students who are the future of the industry and the country."

Family is important, most women agree. It impacts their career choices.

Rachel of Peaks Island, ME, said, "As a single mom I have chosen to work for myself which gives me flexibility with my schedule. I am blessed to have found a community that supports my particular architectural practice. I am in a unique situation, as I live on an island. My work is built locally, but my clients are all over the country. I have managed to weave a creative profession with my number one priority; raising my son."

Rachel of Downing, MO, says her work as a therapist/licensed clinical social worker is immensely rewarding in many ways. "It provides an opportunity to help individuals, couples and families to make positive choices and changes that will strengthen them and help them grow into the direction they want to go in life. To see that happen for them gives me great satisfaction."

Occupational Drawbacks

"If the career you have chosen has some unexpected inconvenience, console yourself by reflecting that no career is without them."

~ Jane Fonda

Many of the drawbacks women mentioned revolved around hours worked and pay level, as well as the absence or limited health plans available on the job.

Elizabeth from WV noted, "There is lots of responsibility and time involved as chief communication officer and legislative liaison. Even when I'm not at work I need to be aware 24/7 of what is going on."

Anita from OK is a personal care attendant. She enjoys the work and helping people but stresses the drawbacks include "low pay and erratic schedules. Plus, often the jobs turn out to be part time and that's very hard. Added to this is the lack of health insurance."

Janet of Winston-Salem, NC, has worked as a medical technologist and an office manager of her husband's ophthalmology practice. "I am a doctor's wife! BAD STIGMA. I have to avoid using his last name, but the staff knows I am not a 'true' doctor's wife."

For Jasmine, Dartmouth, MA, "Working at a nonprofit (The Roger Williams Zoo) necessitates a lifestyle that is within a tight budget with a low salary. In some organizations there is little opportunity to grow. The need to be 'on' every day with teaching kids and present when handling animals (cannot have an 'off' day.)"

Jennifer of Scituate, RI, says her position as manager of the Ambassador Animal Program at the zoo also has salary shortcomings. "It is pretty low considering my degree and that I am the primary breadwinner in the family."

Even though teaching for some is an ideal career choice, others in the profession clearly are aware of its disadvantages.

Heather from Verona, WI, said, "The politics of working in a school are hard sometimes. There's also the fact you can't vacation when you want."

Being a graphic designer means that you have to take other people's ideas and transform them into real projects. However, the reality is that during the process, there is input from many others who may or may not know much about graphic design. Often the designer does not have the last say on the project on which they have worked.

Nancy, from Cleveland, OH, worked as a corporate attorney for five years and is now retired. "My career was in the 1980s and for me the long hours and travel made spending time with my children a real challenge."

Public relations coordinator Marie from Bowling Green, KY, said, "Being a young professional in an industry where so much of your accountability is based on relationships with others in the community can make some things difficult. The lack of age and experience regardless of my two college degrees, multiple internships and previous jobs is a factor that is hard to overcome."

Architectural designer Rachel from Peaks Island, ME, notes the chief drawback of her profession is, "Health insurance and always working is another drawback."

Writer/editor Diane of Anchorage, AK, notes in her position with an engineering firm, "I deal with some unreasonable deadlines, projects get cancelled without notice, which can be frustrating at times."

Caroline from Raleigh, NC, is a bank teller. "My job is highly customer-oriented. Sometimes I feel a lot of pressure and I feel like I'm constantly 'on stage.'"

Lisa from Indianapolis, IN, has also been in banking for 20 years. "It hasn't been fulfilling to me personally. (Soulful, that is). It has been tiring, dirty (handling money) with long hours and weekends and is stressful."

Belinda of Portage, IN, says that at her job as assistant manager of a plaza trade store on a major highway, she enjoys the flexible hours which allows her to care for her children. "But the downside is I've maxed where there is for me to move up career wise."

Pam of Indianapolis, IN, works as a commercial real estate paralegal. "Though it offered great job opportunities, it was 'semi-professional.' I felt I didn't fit in with upper management and don't fit in with support staff. It's been very awkward."

Though owning and operating a New England ski lodge may sound romantic and fun, for the past two decades, Hanna of Rutland, VT, has done just that and all that it entails, including marketing, cooking, cleaning, and hosting, as well as taking reservations and handling improvements of the establishment. "I live above where I work and that can be tiring and boring. Though our apartment is away from the guests, we still feel 'on call' all the time." A former ski instructor from Austria, she misses being able to frequent the slopes as often as she would like. "Running this inn has been wonderful with the people I meet but it's like never having a vacation. It's work all the time."

Lesley of Basking Ridge, NJ, was more concerned about the health-related risks in her business. "I was the owner and instructor of my own dance studio for 33 years. I loved dancing and performing, but the risk for potential injuries always lurked in the back of my mind."

For Bri, who lives in Columbia, MD, a major drawback to her position working in video sales of DVDs is that "people think I do nothing all day and that it doesn't take much to do my job. But it has allowed me to finish college, so how bad is that?"

Jamie of Hernando, MS, agreed with Bri. "I am a telemarketer for a health care provider for diabetics. Many people think I'm just bothering them and hang up. You have to develop a thick skin and not take it personally."

Jessica from North Billerica, MA, who is in sales for a leading dog catalog noted one must be on their best behavior at all times. "All of our calls are recorded and sometimes I feel nervous talking with clients. Occasionally when they play back the calls for us to hear how we interacted; I get really embarrassed because more than once I kept answering 'awesome' to everything the customer said. And one time she said, 'No thanks!'"

When Lenore of Bangor, PA, was only 18 and newly married, she sought out a job where she could sew. "It was a blouse mill just up the street from where we lived. It was really a sweatshop and we were constantly pressured to get the jobs done quickly. It was nerve wracking to say the least."

Several of the women spoke of the physicality of their careers and listed it as a breakdown of their health.

While Dr. Tania of Annapoli, MD, loved her 25 years helping people as a chiropractor, she admitted, "It takes a lot out on your own body."

Massage therapist Tracey of Hackettstown, NJ, said, "It is physically demanding. It can hurt the wrists and the hand and I need to get massage for relief sometimes."

Frances, formerly of Michigan now in Fargo, ND, said her job as a pediatrician has some disadvantages as well. "Being on call all night can be rough if you have your own family to take care of. That was the only thing I didn't like. It's easy to handle when you have no children."

Brie from Clayton, NC, has had several careers: bus driver, owner of a fitness studio, exercise teacher, and substitute teacher. "One of the drawbacks of substituting is that it can be very lonely. Other teachers are not so willing to invite you to talk with them at lunch."

Linda of East Orange, NJ, has been a transit bus driver and notes the negative aspect is that "there is a lot of emotional strain on a driver. You don't know your passengers, but you have to care about them anyway."

Lisa of Flushing, NY, says, "Nursing means a 365 day/24/7 career… never closed…working holidays… inclement weather is no excuse… getting mandated to stay… and in psychiatry: danger, violence, emotional impact beyond that of other nursing settings."

Lynn of Wilmington, DE, is a community photojournalist. "There are unpredictable hours, too much time spent recording names and facts, and we as a group are underpaid."

Working on the hair of a dead person was something that Joyce of Wirtz, VA, took pride in. "I felt I was helping the family see their loved one as they used to be. On one occasion a deceased person was not issued a cause of death. I had to have a Hepatitis shot as a preventative against the disease."

Jean of Sciota, PA, has been a pet groomer for the past decade. "I love animals but one of the drawbacks is that it is very physical work especially handling the larger dogs."

Pamela of Randolph, NJ, works as a pharmacist. "Some of the inconveniences include working holidays and weekends and sometimes patient encounters which can be challenging."

Anita of Great Falls, MT, works as a personal care attendant. "The down side of my job includes low pay, most jobs are just part time with erratic schedules, and importantly the lack of health insurance available from some agencies."

Jamie of Hernando, MS, works for a diabetic product service. "Many people are not so respectful when I call on the phone. They can't seem to realize I am calling with information that could improve their lives. I can get responses from not interested to nasty comments questioning why I am bothering them."

Misperceptions about Jobs

"My reality is the misconception about me."
                                                        ~ *Tori Spelling*

While the future holds promise for computer/technology jobs, there has previously been misperceptions that such fields are not for women. It's been alleged that women feel the sciences are not creative enough.

The women participants to the survey had some interesting observations on the public's notion of their chosen fields. Most of these centered around their salary, the hours worked, and the difficulty of their jobs.

Cindy from Goose Creek, SC, felt that her job as a school bus driver was totally misunderstood. "People think we are crazy or just can't find a good job. Some even think it's the only job we can get because we don't have an advanced education. It's simply not true, at least for me. I really enjoy being with the children."

"People hear that I work at a zoo and immediately assume that I am a zookeeper," said Jasmine of Dartmouth, MA. "They do not realize that one can be an educator and work at a zoo. Also, people think that I just play with kids and show them animals, not realizing that the lesson plans are deliberate and specific to the student's learning needs and standards. They don't get that handling animals takes training and practice. Both aspects of my job are more serious than they seem."

A massage therapist from Clermont, FL, was quite curt in her response. "The public think we deal in the sex trade."

She was not alone. Tracey, a massage therapist in NJ agreed.

Roberta, an operating room nurse from Randolph, NJ, saw a parallel. "In the early days of nursing many single nurses were thought to be 'easy' sexually speaking because we know and see so much of the human body and its nakedness."

Racial bias is still out there as well.

Thelma from Great Falls, MT, is an Indian education coordinator. "There are still misperceptions of people of color that I deal with in my job."

Customer service personnel also get labeled negatively.

Martha from Lenexa, KS, said, "Because I take sales order from catalogs the public thinks I do nothing but sit there all day."

Spring P. from Walls, MS, agrees. In her customer service for a health care company, she claims, "People say we annoy them. We are not there to bug them but to help them. Many of them don't get it and it can be frustrating."

Leah of El Passo, TX works in sales for a major mail order catalog company. "People generally think that all I do is sit around and talk and drink coffee while waiting for orders. Not true. We are always busy whether we are on the phone or not."

The teaching profession has its own branded image.

"People think it's easy to teach," said Lydia, a college professor from Newark, DE. "In some ways it is much harder than anything I've done before. Also there is this perception that all college professors are liberals and they are not."

Another retired teacher from New York, Shirley, hears a different story from critics of teachers. "They say we get too much time off because we don't all work summers. They don't see that if we don't work, we don't get paid."

Speech pathology is different than teaching, but it is a career still within the realm of the educational profession.

Heather from Verona, WI, voiced concern about what the public deems is her job. "They feel we just help kids who can't speak properly regarding sounds; but we also help kids with multiple special needs like Down's syndrome and autism. It's a much broader scope than what we are credited with."

Graphic arts is a career in high demand. With the advances in technology, images need to match the written word. This is true in newspapers, magazines, ad agencies, and public relations firms. Nicole, a graphic designer from Pittsburgh, PA, said, "People think that anyone can draw. That design is easy, fun and effortless and this is far from the way it is."

Elaine is a freelance writer from Ashville, AL. "People assume that you can do what you want, when you want, and your time is your own because you work for yourself. Actually, your time belongs to your editor and you often have to work into the wee hours of the night to get a job done on time."

Say the word "sports," and the public associates it with fun and games. Not so, says Nanette, a disability service sports manager from Surprise, AZ. "I don't just go to games and concerts and have fun. There is ever so much more to my job which includes stress."

Certain careers are seen as glamorous by the public, and this includes working for an airline. Thelma G. from Cary, NC, has worked for 35 years in the customer service-industry agent for two major airlines. "The general public thinks we see beautiful places and meet exciting people and we do. But what they forget is that we have to wait on people on our feet, serve meals, and clean up the aircraft. That's not so glamorous."

The lack of understanding about certain careers occurs in the sciences as well as the arts.

"The public believes that science moves fast and that we make big advances every day," said Tricia from Nashville, TN. An assistant professor of Biomedical Research, she adds, "It just isn't the case."

Money was also an issue that people take for granted in their assumptions about certain occupations.

Sarah, a veterinarian from Chester, NJ, who studied and worked in Scotland, notes, "People call me doctor, but I am not well paid."

According to Janet from Winston-Salem, NC, semantics plays a role in the public's misinformation about the sciences. She is in medical technologies and an office medical manager. "But they think I am a technician. I'm not. Being a technologist with a BS in Bio chemistry is a totally different job."

Joan from Brockton, MA, has been a customer agent for a major wig company. "People think I get free wigs and just goof off all day. That it's not a real job."

Sharon from Minnetonka, MN, also hears the public's misconceptions about her job at an old-fashioned general store. "They think when I'm not ringing up an order or checking stock I just sit and gab with other employees."

Debbie works at a well-known chain restaurant/shop in Arkadelphia, AR. "People think I get clothes or items we stock in the store for free. If I want something, I pay like anyone else."

Mila, a retired pharmacist from Chester, NJ said, "There is a misunderstanding among the public that pharmacists know everything about drugs, meds, drug interactions, side effects and that's not always the case."

Marie of Flanders, NJ, is a retired nurse. "The public think that doctors and nurses have romantic trysts in on-call rooms and closets! It's not like a TV show at all."

Lisa of Flushing, NY is a psychiatric nurse. "The majority of people thing that being a nurse is 'nice' or 'sweet.' We were warned about this before graduating and embarking on our new profession. People have no clue as to the depth of skill and expertise a registered nurse possesses in addition to the paramount need for emotional fortitude, empathy, diplomacy skills, integrity, accountability as things needed to be a nurse. Our role is very misunderstood… even by nurses!"

Lynn, a community photojournalist from Wilmington, DE, noted, "People think the camera does it all and there is little or no personal skill involved."

Jill is a medical coder in Quincy, IL. "The public's most common misperception has to do with the fact that no one seems to know what a 'coder' is."

In West Palm Beach, FL, Judy owns/operates a bakery. "It may sound silly, but people think we are always sampling our goods and eating them while we work. It just isn't so."

Joyce of Wirtz, VA, would always get the same reaction when she told people that she did hair for morticians. "They would say doesn't it bother you that the body is so cold? Or, aren't you afraid of them moving or ghostly presences? I tell them I deal with hair, not the body."

Diane of RI works as the director of marketing/public relations at the Roger Williams Park and Zoo. "People think we just plan parties for the public. Neither of these notions are true."

Not Just One Career Anymore
Multi-tasking Successfully

"Why do they always teach us that it's easy and evil to do what we want and that we need to discipline to restrain ourselves? It's the hardest thing in the world to do what we want. And it takes the greatest kind of courage. I mean, what we really want."

~ Ayn Rand

According to the Bureau of Labor and Statistics, women will change careers throughout their lifetime. This has indicated that the average baby boomer, for example, held 11.7 jobs from the ages of 18-48. In fact, 54.8 percent of the women in the survey noted they have had more than one occupation/career to date compared to 44 percent who had only one career. Included in this latter number are five women who have never held a job outside the home.

No matter how much you like your job, there has probably been a moment of intense drudgery when you stared out the window and imagined becoming a landscape architect or a poetry professor or an attorney or even the driver of an 18-wheel rig. Who doesn't wonder about the paths not taken?

Leaving behind a hard-won first career often means starting over. *Can I really do this now? What if I fail?* These are valid concerns and quite common amongst women who take the gamble. Seeking out a new profession does mean taking financial and emotional risks. But for many women, these new challenges are worth the price.

Why do women leave an established career? For many of the same reasons men do. Frustration and disillusionment and not using their abilities/talents to the fullest are some of the major reasons women leave. Those who work in a diminishing industry want to leave before the rug is pulled out from under them. Others leave as a means of realigning their personal/spiritual values in a mid-life evaluation of their lives.

Stephanie form Hilo, UT, has worked as a bartender, a waitress, and had an office job, but now is a self-described "stay at home mom. Each job had its perks and was right at that time in my life."

"God changed my dream," said dancer Margie of Randolph, NJ. "I really wanted to make a difference and realized performing was only giving them two hours. I went full time serving in performing arts ministry in NY and really wanted to be there to build performers up and make a greater lasting difference in their lives."

Jennifer of Scituate, RI, now works as the manager of Ambassador Animal Programming at Rhode Island's Roger Williams Zoo. "I previously was a bartender and worked in retail management. They were both exhausting, took up too much time and put major strain on the environment."

Making a career switch can be intimidating, but older workers can explore job opportunities that did not exist even as recent as five years ago. This includes in social media, cyber security, financial regulation, and global relations. Teaching and nursing are among the fastest growing occupations for older workers in the coming decades, according to a 2008 survey, "Encore Career" report underwritten by MetLife Foundation and Civic Ventures. It is not uncommon for teachers, nurses, and business women to have new careers as adjuncts or part-time professors in college. And there is more good news. New careers will also be available with employees in demand. For example, The Bureau of Labor Statistics projects the fastest growing careers projected for the years 2016 to 2026 include genetic counselors, physician assistants, solar installers, wind turbine service technicians, and home health aides.

Lynn of Wilmington, DE, was a teacher for 25 years. "I also was a community photojournalist. I was doing both and got tired of teaching so I left."

Judy of West Palm Beach, FL, taught primary grades for a couple of years after college. "I married a man who was a baker in the army and we opened our own shop. I never went back to teaching. In some ways, while raising my two kids it was easier because they could help out and keep busy at the shop after school."

Caldwell, ID, resident Bonnie works now as a cage shift manager in a casino. "I've tried other venues such as banking, data entry and even hospital work. Here I get good benefits and wages. This works best for me right now."

Linda of Plainfield, IN, works as a senior loan operations specialist in a bank. "I had previously worked in restaurant management, but it was too many hours making for very long days."

Layoffs and poor economic trends often lead to a change of careers. Such was the case with Cherry of Rosemont, MN. "I worked as a gate agent at Delta Airlines, but got laid off. I liked it because I am a people-oriented person. Now I work the front desk at a hotel chain and it is an enjoyable job."

Sometimes circumstances are such that our career choices are determined by an event. Margaret of Derry, NH, has worked as a private school teacher, then as a sales associate for a number of years to help pay the bills. "When the business burned down we had to move. But my primary career is an artist and I used to have a gallery in Salem, MA."

When her father passed away, Phyllis of Fountain Valley, CA, took over his hardware store. "I also worked as a receptionist. I became a teacher because I never intended for either job to be a life-long career. Now I am happy in my job."

Different careers work at different times of one's life.

Pat of Arvado, CO, has had a few jobs. "I have worked as a project manager for an electric distributing company, taught at the Y, been a marketing coordinator for an ad agency and a flight attendant for TWA. Each worked for me at that particular time."

Lydia of Newark, DE, spent 22 years as a TV news producer before becoming a professor. "My midlife career change was made a few years ago. I realized that the lifestyle of a top-market producer, while exciting and rewarding in many ways, meant that I was failing in one part of life that turned out to be the most important – my job as a mother. The realization took me completely by surprise, I must admit. Also, I was becoming more and more disgusted with the way in which news and journalism was playing out on screens everywhere. It seemed as though something was missing. I felt that by getting in on the ground floor of training journalists (teaching them) I had a better shot at changing journalism."

For Jeanine of Honolulu, HI, there were advantages to all the jobs she has held in her life. "I was doing accounting work for a while, then I was a speech pathologist and audiologist and then went into real estate. Each position had its perks and downsides."

Diane of Anchorage, AK, said, "I spent six years as an army public relations officer and reported for an army newspaper. I also served one year as installation commander information's officer. Now I write and edit for an engineering firm."

Career Advice

"The most important lesson I think I could impart is don't let anyone determine what your horizons are going to be. You get to determine those yourself. The only limitations are whatever particular talents you happen to have and how hard you're willing to work. And if you let others define who you ought to be, or what you ought to be because they put you in a category, they see your race, they see your gender and they put you in a category. You shouldn't let that happen."
~ Condoleezza Rice

Semi-retired freelance writer Elaine from Ashville, AL, advised young women to "get a college degree in journalism, mass communications or at least in English. Pay attention in English class: know where to place commas, how to pluralize words ending in 's,' know not to dangle a participle phrase. Learn how to write a good lead that will focus your feature and pull your reader in. However, I'm not sure I would council her to start out as freelance writer. She'll need experience first with a newspaper, magazine, ad agency or as a corporate PR person. Once employed, she should do freelance work on the side until she builds a name for herself and accumulates a good portfolio. She shouldn't quit her 'day job' until freelancing is bringing in at least three-fourths of what her full-time employment pays."

Caryn is in project management and lives in Roswell, GA. "I would probably tell a young girl/woman to stay away from IT specifically only because so many companies are using Offshore, it makes it harder to find a job. I don't think you can go wrong with a more general business degree that gives you more flexibility."

Some career advice was amusing.

Bonnie from Caldwell, Idaho works as a cage shift manager at a casino. "I would advise a young person to be careful of carrying heavy bags of money and watch not to relate money going out to customers with a paycheck."

Anita of Great Falls, MT, works as personal care attendant. "I would advise someone thinking about going into the field to be aware that while it is a very rewarding career, you will never get rich doing it."

Diane of South Kingstown, RI, works in public relations and marketing. "I would tell a young woman to explore all the options. Get as much experience in a variety of communications disciplines including writing and pitching stories as well as social media and event planning. Try a public relations and/or marketing agency first – it is a fast and fun world."

Mila of Chester, NJ, is a retired pharmacist. "I would tell any women considering the profession to go for it. At present, this is a much-needed profession around the world. It is a great career for women."

Liz, a retired former administrative assistant from Westbrook, CT, noted, "Do this career only if you are in an organization that offers upward opportunities or you begin your own business. You must enjoy service-oriented work."

Financial remuneration was mentioned frequently in the advice women in the survey noted.

"Go into higher education and don't limit yourself to the position of administrative specialist," said Lisa of Stratford, CT, who speaks from her experiences.

Lynn of Wilmington, DE, has been employed as a community photojournalist. "I would counsel a young woman not to seek this as a profession if she needs to support herself."

Lydia of Newark, DE, advises young women who want to be a professor to "not stay in grad school. Go out and get a job, get experience. Then when you go back to school for graduate work, you have something upon which to base your teaching. If you want to go into journalism DO it! But don't expect a lot of money or time off. If you have a passion and fire in your belly to be a journalist you can do it."

Internships are a great way to get a glimpse into what a specific field is like.

Jeanine who lives in Honolulu, HI, and has worked as a realtor said, "I would tell the young girls really try to get in contact and do actual day to day work alongside a professional. Be with him or her every day and see what goes on. Real estate is a lot harder than I ever thought; lots more classes. There are so many hours of credits per year to keep your license active and set quotas you must meet in a year. Try it on for size before you commit."

Lisa from Indianapolis, IN, has worked in the banking industry for 17 years. "If a young girl has a love of business things, numbers and of course people, this could be very satisfying. She could move up and make more money quickly if she has energy and lots of confidence."

Lisa from Flushing, NY, advises young women thinking of going into nursing: "Don't! Given the current state of healthcare, even if I thought the person was cut out for it, I'd never recommend it (they'd never forgive me!!!) And I'd reserve sharing my opinions if they were already in school so as not to cause them distress or adversely affect their success."

An elementary school teacher for over 20 years, Phyllis of Fountain Valley, CA, said, "I would tell a young woman it is a great gig and it is very rewarding but it has become very competitive and difficult to get jobs so patience will be required."

Derry, NH, resident Margaret has been a preschool teacher. "I would tell a young girl considering going into preschool education that she needs to teach the children to obey her first before she expects to attain their affection. There can be no love without first earning respect. So many come into the job thinking it all will be 'fun.' They think it's play time all day without realizing the hard work it is to actually TEACH."

Burnout is sometimes a result of working in the educational field.

Shirley of E. Syracuse, NY, who has taught deaf children notes, "Teaching has become very stressful, too much paperwork, too much control and too many restrictions."

Margie of Randolph, NJ, has been a musical theater performer. "I would advise any young woman thinking of pursuing theater to not compromise herself for any paying job and remain a woman of integrity, honesty and a great team player who stays passionate!"

Alysia of San Pedro, CA, does telemarketing. She is also attending classes to become a medical assistant. "Some people think, incorrectly, that this job is a forever job for many women who have no training or experience. That isn't always the case. Women considering a career might think about telemarketing as a way to earn money while continuing their studies. It helps pay for books and some tuition and you don't need to have an advanced education to do it. It can be a great stepping stone to your final goals."

Belinda is an assistant manager of a daycare at a trade store on a highway in Portage, IN. "Don't go into this job," she advises. "Don't raise other people's kids."

Succeeding and earning advancement in any position requires some sacrifices. Linda, of Plainfield, IN, said this has been true in her job as a banker. "Success, advancement and raises are given to those who volunteer and go above and beyond to be considered for promotion," she advises.

Another bank employee, Linda from Indianapolis, IN, suggests that women should "choose a career that is more fulfilling. There are so many more career opportunities for the younger generation that would give them a more meaningful outlook on the type of work they can do on a day to day basis."

Marie, a publicist in Bowling Green, KY, disclosed the inside scoop on working in her field. "Be open-minded and never assume you'll know what the day will bring. It's always different. And that can be a good thing."

Positions in the social service field can be rewarding but difficult as well. Rachel of Downing, MO, is a clinical therapist. "It is challenging. Every day is different and entails a high degree of responsibility. But one also needs to beware of compassion fatigue and the client is the expert philosophy. Also there are many barriers to overcome."

Working at the right job at the right time benefits many women, such as Sara Lynn of Dakota City, NE, who worked as a waitress. "The tips are good and it has been a really good job while I was taking college classes."

Veterinarian Sarah from Chester, NJ, recommends women, "do it because you love it, because you can't ever imagine your life doing anything else. Get ready for blood, sweat and tears and a lack of what it's okay to talk about in public."

Lesley of Flanders, NJ, owned and taught at a dance studio. "Go with your heart but understand the financial difficulties involved in this career unless you are a star and not many achieve that status."

Glamour is not the only attraction a career offers. In many cases, it's the money that matters. And sometimes, it's also the satisfaction of doing a job that previously was only done by men.

Amanda of Hackettstown, NJ, notes that her job cleaning septic tanks may not be alluring, but it has taught her many things. "I would tell a woman considering this not to shy away from hard work or getting dirty and also not to let anyone push her around. This is a male-driven field so there will be times when people want to say inappropriate things to and about you. There are also times when the competition feels threatened by a female in the field. It doesn't happen often, but it does happen."

Certain positions demand emotional strength. Crisis support specialist, Kathy, from Randolph, NJ, warns, "This is a job that is not for the faint hearted."

Freelance graphic designer Linda from New York City, NY notes, like most careers in the arts, you have to be passionate about it or you would be wasting your time trying to light a fire without a spark. Do it for the love of it because the salaries are rarely great."

Honing in on only one aspect of a job isn't always the best idea. For example, project manager inside a sales division, Jackie of Brownsville, PA, advised a woman considering her position "to be as diversified as possible in your skill set. Take advantage of all training and company benefits offered by the employer for college or technology school training. Learn skills not required of your current position and keep up with trends in technology such as computer skills. Offer to assume and learn new responsibilities and training within your company or department."

Proprietorship – being the boss – isn't always an easy situation. One cannot rest on their past performance and staying on top of trends is a vital part of maintaining a good and thriving business.

Barbara, who owns her own salon in Nazareth, PA, said, "People like change, so you need to keep up with current hair styles and colors."

Lyneta of Spring Hill, TN, is a writer. Her advice? "Get a journalism or English degree but also take a variety of interesting classes that have nothing to do with writing such as history, anthropology and political science to make for a well-rounded writer."

Certain jobs in the medical field offer a number of options which attract lots of women like Janet of Winston Salem, NC, who has worked as a medical technologist. "It's a great career. It is stable, good benefits and you have the choice to work in a hospital or a doctor's office."

Gender Parity: Fair Play?

"I want to be paid for the work that I'm doing. That's what every single woman around the world wants. We want to be paid on parity with a man in a similar position."
~ Felicity Jones

American women who work full time in the marketplace are paid 80 cents for every dollar earned by men. While the Equal Pay Act (EPA) has been in existence for 50 years, there still remains a wage gap between the genders. Good news: there is now a proposed US Labor Law, The Paycheck Fairness Act (S. 819, H.R. 1869), which would update and strengthen the EPA in important ways.

Research including, the April, 2017 Pew Research Center, indicates that pay discrepancies between men and women are most obvious in five particular jobs. These include sales consultants, with a difference of 27 percent in pay. Experts allege that beside skill and education, a main focus is placed on a certain type of personality. According to Pew Research, women's earnings were 83 percent of men's in 2015. The differences between which determines success, and success is not easily measurable.

With the real estate market, there is a 23 percent difference between genders in jobs as a real estate broker. According to Amy Tennery, managing editor of *The Jane Dough*, a website that examines the business world from a female point of view, real estate is regularly named among the most discriminatory fields for women. One factor listed as a possible reason for the discrepancy is the hours worked beyond the traditional 40-hour work week. Perhaps men are putting in a lot more hours than women.

Thirdly, women account for 62 percent of those who work as recruiting directors working with human resources department. Yet women earn 20 percent less on average than their male counterparts.

The job of a portfolio manager still exemplifies a 15 percent parity between what women and men in the same position earn. One reason might be the fact that men make up 74 percent of those in the finance jobs. Experts in the field say this may be changing in view of the wake of the financial crash when risky trading now seems a liability and stereotypes of women being "cautious" may turn out to be a benefit in the long term.

Finally, the position of CEO, Chief Executive Officer, has been male monopolized by this high paying career for decades. Men in this position represent 79 percent of corporate heads and earn 15 percent more than women in the same position.

Tennery states, "This one hurts – but it's all too true. Without a critical mass in the CEO field, it's tough for women to lobby for equal pay."

Yet the field is slowly changing. Do you recognize the names of these women? Mary Barra, CEO of General Motors; Ginni Romelty, CEO of IBM; Indra Nooyi, CEO of PepsiCo; and Marillyn Hewson, CEO of Lockheed Martin.

Knowing all this are the women in this survey where they want to be?
It depends on the career and the experience one has. The majority of women in the survey said they did not think there was a major difference in the pay for men and women doing the same job.

Alysia of San Pedro, CA, notes that her telemarketing company hires a lot more women. "They sound better on the phone, we're told, but I'm not sure there is a pay difference."

Several educators were adamant that "there are definitely pay differences between male and female teachers. Lisa of Stratford, CT, notes that "it's especially true when it comes to getting the administrative jobs."

Jeanine from Honolulu, HI, has worked in accounting, speech pathology audiology, and real estate. "There is no pay difference between men and women in speech therapy because it is a civil service job nor in real estate. However, in accounting there were men who were definitely paid more."

One of Sheila's jobs was working in a Home Depot. The Tannersville, PA, resident said, "Absolutely the men there got paid more than the women."

Many participants in the survey said while there was not always a difference in pay, there was a more obvious difference in the promotions received by men and women.

Nancy, a retired corporate attorney from Cleveland, OH, said, "I don't think there is a discrepancy with a job, but I think it is still more challenging for women to be promoted especially to the highest levels."

Linda of Indianapolis, IN said, "As history would have it in the work force, it has been known for years and to this day that men have always earned more than women. That is not to say that women have come a really long way, but in my personal opinion, there will always be a discrepancy in earnings in the workforce."

Business banker/commercial lender Kelly of Slidell, LA, voiced the opinion that, "I don't know personally of any financial discrepancies between what men and women get paid. However, I have heard that men earn a good bit more in the same position."

Tricia of Nashville, TN, is an assistant professor in Biomedical Research. "Salary surveys in my field indicate a 10 percent difference between what men and women earn."

There has always been a significant fiscal inequity between the profit and not-for-profit markets. The answer is simple: a nonprofit organization uses its surplus revenues to further achieve and enhance its mission rather than distribute its income to its shareholders as profits. As a result, wages are lower than jobs in the for-profit sector. Working in a national or state park, certain funded day care centers and public zoos are some examples of the non-profit niche.

Jennifer, Scituate, RI, noted, "I'm not aware of any difference in pay for gender. The field – non-profit zoo –is pretty low paying across the board for everyone."

Relationships: How Do They Rate?

"I wonder how many people don't get the one they want, but end up with the one they're supposed to be with?"
~ Fannie Flagg

The National Opinion Research Center at the University of Chicago found that in 2014, 60 percent of people reported being "very happy" in their personal relationships. This was actually down from 65 per cent in 2012.

When it comes to the positivity of their relationships, it seems that the younger the woman, the more satisfied she is with her partner. Familiarity, it seems, at least via long-term relationship, ebbs in terms of fulfillment and happiness.

Women were asked to rate their relationship on a scale of zero to 10, with those scoring 0 to 5 as being "poor" and or 6 to 10 being "excellent." Contrary to many news reports that fewer couples stay together, only 37 percent of the women rated their marriages and long-term relationships as relationship as "poor" or "bad." Conversely, those offering a rating of six to 10 represented a whopping 63 percent. An additional 9.2 percent opted not to answer this question.

The percentage of married women who participated in the survey was 53 percent; when asked, what you would change about your relationship, the majority responded: "communicate more."

Women had many reasons for ranking their relationships on the lower end of the scale. They explained not helping with housework or child rearing, not holding a sustainable job, in- law issues, drinking, infidelity, gambling, and not supporting their own career choices. Others cited age differences, opposing life interests, and health issues as detriments to a more positive relationship.

Responses varied from those who said they made a mistake marrying their husband in the first place, to those who were just tired of coping. A few women, like Pat from Arvada, CO, had been married 15 years. "How would I have changed things? Never marry him in the first place."

Nannette of Surprise, AZ, was on the same page. She was married for six years and is now divorced. "Looking back I would rate our relationship with a 2. It was very one-sided with me constantly trying to make the relationship work, mainly for the kids and eventually it was a losing battle."

Some women directly attributed the failure of their marriage to very specific causes.

Caroline from Great Falls, MT, has been divorced for 25 years. Rating her marriage a 4, she explained, "If I could change the relationship, I would have found a way to keep my husband from drinking and fooling around with women."

CT resident Lisa said her marriage dissolved nine years ago. She said she had been warned but didn't heed what she was told. "I never should have married him. Should have listened to everyone."

The adults in a marriage often change over the years. Such was the case with Linda from Plainfield, IN, whose relationship ended after six years. "My partner changed very much after the marriage and I'm not sure how I could have changed that."

Lisa from Indianapolis rates her 13-year marriage with a 4.5. "I would marry a younger man (my husband is 12 years my senior) and have stood up for what I needed instead of thinking it was selfish. I wish I'd believed more in myself by having children made a priority."

Everyone knows domestic bliss is not guaranteed. But most of us hope that violence is not a part of a good partnership as well.

Katora of CT rated her relationship a 1. I should have never chosen him. He was a cheat and threw my son and I out of the house. It was very tough."

Jeanine of Honolulu, HI, has been widowed but says her relationship was a 5. "I would have put my foot down regarding so many things with his brother in the business and insisted he not do it. I would have opened my mouth more and forged my husband's signature while his brother was still alive."

Some women were beyond solutions of improving their relationships. Neva from Des Moines, WA, scores her marriage a low ranking of 4. "At this point I would do nothing to change it."

More upbeat were comments by women like Elaine from Ashville, AL, married for 26 years before being widowed. She rated her marriage a 9.5. "It was really wonderful."

Though Amanda from SD is single, she rates her current relationship an 8. "If I could change anything, I would want him to be more mature as he is the father of our twin boys."

Elementary school teacher Gloria, who has dual residences in Connecticut and Vermont, was married for seven years before she lost her husband. Rating their relationship as a 7, she said, "I would be less compliant if I could change that relationship."

Heather from Verona, WI, has been married 15 years and scores her relationship a 6. "I would try to be more attractive to the guy. He's a good dad and helps around the house when I nag him. It's like siblings living together. I'd try to get passion back in life."

Elizabeth from WV is married 31 years and offers a score of 8. Her solution? "Less work, more play and more time for friends, could improve it."

Newlyweds have a different take on the scoring. Stephanie from Hill, UT, rates her marriage a 10. "I wouldn't change a thing about our relationship."

From east to west, there were echoes of satisfaction from women. Margaret of Derry, NH has been married for 44 years and gives it "a solid 10. I do wish my husband would take more of an interest in athletic activities like golf or biking with me.

Cindy, from Goose Creek, SC, said of her husband, "I wish he'd talk more."

Diane from Randolph, NJ, has been married twice. "The first time was for 16 years and I rate it a 2; the second marriage is 29 years and I rate it with an 8. I wish my husband wasn't so involved with the dog and could do more things with me during the day."

The pendulum on the positivity of marriage swings both ways. Tricia from Tennessee has been married for 10 years and rated her relationship as a 10. "How would I change it? Add more hours in the day to be together every day."

Deda, from Bayonne, NJ, says of her four year relationship, " It's a 10 and great. I wouldn't change anything in my relationship."

"The beginning of our 18-year marriage rated a six," said Indianapolis, IN, resident, Linda. "Now that we are divorced – 13 years – I look back and think if I could go back in time, the changes I would make is to be more concerned about the quality of the person that I am choosing as a partner rather than looking to get the title of being married. This person does not need to be wealthy (although it wouldn't hurt) just have a job that pays decent wages and have a true relationship with God. I think if these characteristics are there, everything else will fall into place."

Rose of Netcong, NJ, is 91 years old. A retired insurance broker, she was widowed a few years ago. "On a scale of one to 10 I would give our marriage a 10. We got along beautifully."

Relationships: What Could Be Improved?

> "Chains do not hold a marriage together. It is threads, hundreds of tiny threads which sew people together through the years."
> ~ *Simone Signoret, French cinema actress often hailed as one of France's greatest film stars (She became the first French person to win an Academy Award, for her role in* Room at the Top.*)*

It's been often said that married people live longer than those who are single. If nothing else, this hope for the extension of our health and lives is certainly one that deserves consideration. This leads many of us to wondering if there exists a magic potion to rekindle and/or transform tired or broken long-term relationships.

In a study, "The Ambiguous Link Between Marriage and Health," published online in the journal *Social Forces* 2017, sociologist Matthijs Kalmijn reported findings from the Swiss Household Panel, a 16-year survey of more than 11,000 Swiss adults. Contrary to popular thinking, the people in this survey reported slightly worse health than when they were single. And with time, their health did not improve. In essence, marriage had no impact on men or women's' health.

In our survey, women ranked their marriages from 1 to 10; one being very poor, 10 equaling excellent. All women suggested ways of improving. Not surprisingly, many women voiced the need for better or more communication.

Many women emphasized this factor as the main reason for their separation and ultimate divorce. Rather than talking together, some men will pursue a hobby, watch TV sports, or even read.

Sue of Randolph, NJ, provided one such example: "My husband is an avid reader. I read too, but he's always reading and pays no attention to me. When I pause from my book and say something he doesn't respond. It's like I'm not even there."

Of her second 13-year marriage, Elizabeth of Westbrook, CT, said, "It needs improvement, but I can't change it, so I live with it."

Linda of Indianapolis, IN, said she had some ideas how to make it better. "I know this sounds crazy, but actually slowing down and taking time to listen and talk to each other is something we could improve. We are so busy, we just don't take the time to listen or pay much attention to each other."

Of those women who rated their marriage 1 to 6, on the lower end of the scale, time, money, and appreciation were issues mentioned as a detriment to their relationships. Many cited work, children, and older adult care as impediments to their division of time they could spend with their significant other.

Introspection of their own contributions or lack thereof was also mentioned by a few responders. Barbara of Nazareth, PA, has been married 45 years. "I guess if I could change anything, it would be myself. I am too giving and caring to my whole family and they need to do more to be helpful to me."

Lydia of Newark, DE, rated her 22 year-relationship as a five. "To improve the relationship I would have been more vocal about my needs and expectations early on in the relationship."

For Sheila of Tannerville, PA, "I would rate our marriage a 9 out of 10. What I would change is the amount of time we spend together."

For Jasmine, Dartmouth, MA, time and distance needed improvement. "I wish we had lived closer and that he had more time/energy to give to me."

Women who rated their partners on the higher end of the spectrum, 7 to 10, indicated little or no room for improvement.

Bonnie of Caldwell, ID, has been married for 15 years. "I wouldn't change a thing," she said.

Diane of South Kingstown, RI, said, "I have a great marriage – a 10. If we could change anything it would be work less and spend more time together traveling."

Nannette of Surprise, AZ, said, "I think in any later-in-life relationship, both parties carry baggage from their past. They both have hurts and may find it hard to start trusting again. I was single and completely closed off from even the thought of dating for over five years. I have had two failed long-term relationships and want to be cautious about going back into patterns of co-dependency and enabling. I am stubbornly independent and am still learning that it's okay to rely on someone else… not to 'Complete Me' but to enhance my life."

Help around the house was an area that needs improvement for Phyllis of Fountain Valley, CA. Designating her marriage an 8, she added, "I wish my husband would have better follow through on things he says he is going to do."

Others declined to cite specific reasons other than comments such as, "I should have never married him," according to Lisa of Stratford, CT.

"I could improve our relationship by moving back to NJ," said Vicky of DE. "That's where my closest friends are and I really miss them."

Linda of Clermont, FL, said, "What would improve our relationship is to have the same days off."

Several women like Lois of Fairplay, CO and Tania of Annapolis, MD said, "We would change nothing about our relationship."

As people age, they change. Not always for the better and not always in step with their partner over a period of time. Such was the case with Rachel, Peaks Island, ME, who explained, "When it was good it was an 8. When it was bad it was -10. The relationship was unchangeable due to mental illness involved."

Carlene of Great Falls, MT, said, "I wish I could have found a way to keep him from drinking and fooling around."

Katora of CT said, "I should never have chosen him. There could not have been any improvement in the situation. He was a cheat and threw my son and I out of the house. That was the end."

Some women realized there does not exist a perfect marriage and have learned to adapt to changes. "I can't change things now. I just learn to live with it," Elizabeth of Westbrook, CT.

Belinda of Portage, IN, said she, "Wish I left the marriage earlier."

Pat of Sandyston, NJ, commented that, "Our relationship went from a 10 to a 4. He eventually drank a quart of gin a day, would not take a job because he said he had to be an entrepreneur. I left."

Widow Kelly of Slidell, LA, said, "I wish we had spent more time together."

Some women say there are always signs of a marriage that is going downhill.

"I would have listened to the warning signs," said Anita of Great Falls, MT.

Children and Parenting

"If you bungle raising your children I don't think whatever else you may do matters much."

~ *Jacqueline Kennedy*

Forty years ago, when women graduated from high school and college, many felt obligated to marry and start a family. With the passage of time, women who were not married feared their biological clock was ticking so loudly that children did not seem an option. Things have certainly changed.

In the survey, 26.2 percent of the women had no children; 16.3 percent had one child; 49.1 percent had two to four children; and 5.7 percent had between five and 10 children. Many were over 30 when they had their first child, so that initial worry of the 50s has been put to rest.

Another big change of the times is that no matter the age of the responder, generally speaking, the women did not feel motherhood is mandatory to have a successful, happy life. Adoption and same gender parenting were also an issue not off the table for most of the participants.

Linda from Clermont, FL, explained her thoughts. "Just because you are a female does not mean you HAVE to procreate. I think some women have children because they think they are supposed to. You have to have a yearning and desire and be willing to sacrifice EVERYTHING!"

"I don't care a bit that I never had children," said Pat of Sandyston, NJ. "If I had I would have been up the creek without a paddle!"

Caroline of Great Falls, MT, has five children. "I don't think all women should have children. Women are finally starting to realize they do have choices."

Raising a child alone no longer carries the stigma it once did. The majority of women had no morality issues with single parenting, save for the financial strain which many have due to the fact the father was not in the picture.

Roxanne of UT felt positive about single parenting. "I gave birth to my five children and my ex walked out when the youngest was four. I raised them on my own with no child support from him."

Jennifer of Scituate, RI called single moms, "My heroes. Having children is totally up to the women. My partner works away from home half of the week and it is so hard without him!"

Same gender parenting is more recognized as acceptable than ever before but there were women who still had opposition.

Jackie from Brownsville, PA, said, "I believe a family is composed of a father and mother. Same gender couples create difficulties for the children interacting with family and friends. This creates unnecessary pressure for the children. There are enough couples – male/females wanting to adopt and these children should be given the benefit of this kind of family structure."

Kelly from Slidell, LA is more torn. "I am very traditional in my attitude toward family units. But, I have a gay sister and think that if she and her partner wanted children together, I wouldn't want them denied that opportunity, although I think it can be difficult for the children."

Some women who were raised very religiously, were openly opposed to such parenting. Anita of Great Falls, MT, the mother of three children, disagrees with same sex parenting. "Same sex couples are a direct violation of God's law and against Biblical teachings. Children thrive best with heterosexual parents."

Rebecca of West Plains, MO, was also not in favor of gay parenting. "I do not recommend gays having children because look at every society in every country where the family breaks down. It's not too long before all of civilization does."

Elizabeth of Beckley, WV said, "I do not endorse gender couples specifically referring to 'gay' marriages who want children."

"I have no problem with alternative families," said Janet of Winston-Salem, NC. "It is society that may have a problem. I am a live and let live kind of person."

Jasmine of Dartmouth, MA, has no children though she hopes to someday. "Everyone who wants to be a parent should have the option to, including couples or individuals of any gender or orientation. We all have the capacity to love and nurture and share our life knowledge and there are so many children who need that. I do feel however, that not all women should have children. One of the reasons I do not have any is because we are overpopulated on this planet already. I am considering fostering or adopting. I think single parenting is the bravest thing a person can do and I greatly admire that."

Religious or Spiritual

"Belief doesn't rest on proof or existence...it rests on faith... without faith there is nothing."
~ *Colleen McCullough,* **The Thorn Birds**

I remember when I was a child, if someone accusatorily asked, "Did you swipe that?" I would be mortified thinking they implied I was stealing. Today, we go to an ATM or inside to a bank teller and she asks us to "swipe" our card. Words in our world can easily change meaning.

The same is true when it comes to religion. The women I spoke with were split on formal organized religious participation and an individual's spiritual unity with God. Those of the latter belief saw no difference in their "religiosity," asserting you don't have to go to a special building to communicate with your maker.

A survey by the Pew Forum on Religion and Public Life details the religious affiliation of the American public and explores the shifts taking place in the country's religious landscape. Based on interviews with 35,000 Americans 18 and over, Pew's survey finds religion divertive and extremely fluid. More than 28 percent of all adults have left the faith in which they were raised in favor of another religion or no religion at all. In addition, the number of people unaffiliated with any faith is 16.1 percent, more than double the numbers who say they were not affiliated with any religion as a child. Among those 18-29, one in four say they practice no religion at all.

So where do our women stand? According to the survey, 39.2 percent described themselves as "very religious," while 24 percent assumed the label of "somewhat religious." Another 12.6 percent said they were not active in "formalized or organized religion," but instead acknowledged they were "spiritual" in their beliefs. Finally, 24 percent claimed they were "not at all" religious.

An interesting note is that even those who proclaimed themselves "religious," there was still a degree of moderation in their outright practices and attitudes/toleration towards the beliefs or non-beliefs of others.

"Religion is very important to me," said Linda of Indianapolis, IN. "Even though I was made to go to church since a young age, I understand the benefit of it since I am an adult. My belief is when there is nothing that makes any sense and life seems hopeless, you must have a relationship with someone higher and more powerful than any earthly being. Even though it means that we live by faith and not by sight, sometimes, this is all you need to make it through difficult times and to just to keep you going daily. I do believe everyone should have their own relationship with God or whomever or whatever they chose to worship."

Mila of Chester, NJ, classifies herself as "very religious. Since childhood I was very involved heavily in all church activities in the Philippines where I was born, including charities, committees, fundraising, instruction, etc. Now in my golden years I'm involved in only three or four activities."

Though she observes the laxity of current Christmas celebrations amongst the general population, Joyce of Wirtz, VA, said, "Religion is still my mainstay and I am involved in church functions."

East coast or West coast, there are women with strong beliefs in their church. Neva of Des Moines, WA, said, "Religion is very important. I am active in charities and committees and camps for the church."

Deep in the heart of Texas, some women are very religious and passionate about their beliefs and practices.

"Prayer is a daily thing for me," noted Cheryl of Bandera, TX.

Lynetta of Spring Hill, TN, is very involved in her church. "I teach Bible studies, serve as communion host, and speak for women's events occasionally. I've also served in children's ministry and choir over the years."

Jill of Quincy, IL, said "Religion is very important to me as well as educating my children about God."

Judy of Indian Land, SC, claims religion is "very important to me. I am a better person because I believe in God and want to do the right thing to please Him and make Him proud of me. I do not myself believe in *organized* religion, but feel it is necessary for most people. I was brought up Catholic and then became a Born Again Christian and I am spiritual. I go every week to a small Bible Study group with 10 other women. I also attend Women's Fellowship when I can. I observe that religion is more prevalent and important in the South. I live in the Bible belt and am proud of it."

Linda of Plainfield, IN, noted, "I've always been religious. The degree has varied during different phases of my life, but I'm still religious."

Personal events can have an impact on the degree of spirituality a woman practices. "Religion was the driving force of my life because my brother died without baptism," said Kathryne of Flanders, NJ. "I had to know his soul was safe."

As far as going beyond just attending services, Rehba of Cincinnati, OH, is proud of her work in the church. "Religion is infused in all of my life and has been since childhood. I worship publicly weekly, teach church school, serve as an officer in church, and am in the choir and in the many spiritual activities offered. There is no life without religion for me."

"My husband is the pastor of a small church," said Elizabeth of WV. "We attend services three times a week."

For Margaret of Derry, NH, "I support the others in my group in their pursuit of faith, I go to Catholic mass every Sunday, attend Bible studies, help out with church faire, was in the choir and am a proud member of the Tabernacle Society."

Interpreting the concept of "keeping the faith" is not clear. In some cases, aging and empty nesters ease up on full blown celebrations. For example, Ellen of Mt. Arlington, NJ, said, "I was raised in a Jewish house. I observe holidays and keep up the traditions but I do not actively participate."

And then are the women who say they are not at all religious, but spiritual in their beliefs.

"I was raised as a Quaker but was never really religious, but secular humanist only. Later I became a Unitarian/Universalist which is much the same," said Pat from Sandyston, NJ.

"I have beliefs that don't fit in a structure," said Janet of Winston-Salem, NC. "I go to church and am involved as I can with working. It does not run my life, it is a guide."

"I live a spiritual practice and a life of contemplation," explained Rachel of Peaks Island, ME. "I am a yogi and meditation practitioner."

Barbara of East Syracuse, NY, had a similar reaction. "I would not use the word 'religion' to describe that aspect of my life. I am a deeply spiritual woman in the Christian faith tradition. My faith gives my life purpose."

Jeanine of Honolulu, HI, admits she is "more spiritual than religious. To me religion is strict Catholic Church. I changed to a Christ church and enjoy the services. I do volunteer work and take classes to become a licensed unity teacher."

Many women seem to take a humanistic approach to their spirituality. Lisa of Indianapolis, IN, said, "Religion per se is not as important to me as it is to have a sense or belief in the soul and respect of others souls no matter their lot in life."

Although she identifies herself as a Christian, Bonnie of Caldwell, ID, explained, "I don't necessarily believe in churches. Parents taught us we all live under God's roof."

"Religion is not as important to me as spirituality," according to Lorraine of Hackettstown, NJ. Is there a difference between the two? "Yes, religion is manmade; spirituality is your relationship with God."

And then there were those who said they were in no way religious. Some voiced the obvious hypocrisy of some church goers who put on a different façade in church than when they are not in church.

"If you mean religious by attending church and following all their rules and regulations, that is not very important to me," said Gail of Magnolia, DE. "I enjoy attending church to connect with other Christians and to hear the word of God. Anyone can go to church and get involved in all kinds of activities to make themselves feel good. I believe there is a difference between religion and faith. You can have one without the other. Go to church and walk out the door and treat people like dirt. Faith is believing in God and following your heart based on the teachings of the Bible. I would much rather share my story of the day I was born again than to be involved in religious mumbo jumbo."

The geography of women did not seem to indicate a clear delineation between believers and non-believers.

Nicole of Pittsburgh, PA, claims, "Religion has no importance to me."

Elizabeth of Westbrook, CT agreed. "Not religious at all."

Those women who had already raised their children also tended to visit church less frequently and called themselves "somewhat" religious.

"I don't go much now that my kids are grown up," said Lynn of Wilmington, DE.

Linda of Clermont, FL said, "I don't believe I have to go to church to prove my religious beliefs. I do believe in God and I can talk to him every day. I am not off on Sundays and can't make it to church, so I have my own services with God anytime, anywhere."

It didn't seem to matter what religion a woman was raised in when it comes to how she observes her spirituality as an adult. For example, Melanie of West Jordan, UT, described herself as "a non-practicing Mormon."

"Religion is really not important at all for me," Amanda of Rapid City, SD.

Tricia of Nashville, TN, echoed similar sentiments. "Religion is not a big part of my life. Occasionally I will attend a Unitarian/Universalist church service."

Jennifer of Sciate, RI, said, "Religion is not at all important to me."

Women who responded to the survey mentioned their one time or ongoing participation in the Roman Catholic Church, various Protestant denominations, the Jewish faith, Unitarian and Universal practices.

"I am a pagan," said Jasmine of Dartmouth, MA. "It is important to me. I do not actively practice, yet it is a core part of my self-identity. I am not involved in any organized religions."

Morality: A Bankrupt Commodity?

"The right way is not always the popular way. Standing for right when it is unpopular is a true test of true character."
~ Margaret Chase Smith

In 2015, 72 percent of Americans (male and female) said they believed that US morals were on a downward spiral. Of those, 45 percent classified these morals as "poor." So said the respondents to Gallup's "Annual Values and Beliefs" report.

The report attributed this decline due to the fractured notion of the traditional family with many parents not married or absent from the relationship; the change of curriculum within the pubic school system, "focusing less on American History, grammar, literature and the arts and more on what the *National Review* (4/7/15) called social justice, environmental issues, and sex."

Many women interviewed believe that the world has changed so much and that morality has plummeted. Their reasoning is logical, if not positive. As each generation accepts different morals the old ones are being replaced and society, according to some, erodes, while others view this as progressive.

Examples include pre-marital sex in the 50s and 60s, where unwed mothers and single parenting were considered out-of-the-box behavior. Today, such customs are readily accepted. When Nathaniel Hawthorne penned his *Scarlet Letter*, branding Hester Prynne with a scarlet A for adultery in the 19th century, it was a cultural shock, even a sin. Today's adulterers get counseling, try to heal, or divorce. Much has admittedly changed. Abortion is no longer an impediment to women's health or status and more options loosen morals.

Smoking cigarettes in 1912 was immoral. Today, women who choose not to do so for health reasons and those who are not ashamed to defy medical advice and smoke are no longer considered odd. Back then, contraception was not readily available, and now it's considered by many a "right."

It is logical to assert then, that morality changes as society changes, and many things once labeled "immoral" are now accepted. So if all these changes are acceptable, why did so many of the women in the survey maintain that our collective morality is on a descending path?

Amanda of Rapid City, SD, was firm in her response. "People are creepy. They often take the easy way out. For example, they put kids on meds, don't spank or discipline them, but resort to medicating them."

Perception, as we all know, is in the eye of the beholder. People "seem" to fit into certain moral categories in accordance with their characteristics and behavior. Throughout the ages the older generations carry the sentiment that things were different when they were growing up. Alyssia of San Pedro, CA, stated, "I have morals. Today's young people don't."

Stephanie of Hill, UT, also voiced concern regarding child rearing. "I see a breakdown in morality because parents are just not doing a good job in raising their kids."

Joyce of Wirtz, VA, said, "Gosh, yes there's a breakdown. People don't have true faith in God and his laws. We push God out of schools. What can you expect?"

Cheryl of Bandera, TX, attributes the declining morality as a consequence of "too much technology. There is too much of a need for instant gratification instead of working toward a goal. It has to come instantly for some young people. My generation was not like that."

Neva of Des Moines, WA, concurred. "Too many gadgets/games to take attention away from family time. Families need to connect and eat together."

Juliana of Double Star, WY, said she sees "a huge breakdown in the 20 to 35 year old people who have no morals and generational shift in child rearing."

Diane of Randolph, NJ, says, "It seems like anything goes. When I was young, there were many more morality concerns and we lived with our parents until we got married. In some ways, I would have preferred today's freedoms and choices, but the disadvantage of the times is that it takes young people much longer to grow up."

Mary of Albuquerque, NM, said, "I definitely see a breakdown in present day America. I attribute it to a younger generation of children not having to work for what they want. A car, cellphone, clothes all of these wants are taken care of by their parents without any responsibility for chores."

Linda of NYC is in agreement. "I often question why the breakdown of morality is occurring. If the answer was clear it may be possible to reverse it. But I tend to think it is the breakdown in the family. Combined with pressure from society, media, advertising and technology to acquire more, work harder, buy the latest fashions, the bigger houses, people are distancing themselves from each other to become better consumers. 'Better consumers' is a good term to compare people to ant colonies. They become a part of the GDP machine and miss seeing the joy in the world around them."

Jasmine of Dartmouth, MA, had a different take on the subject. "I am saddened at the heightened polarity of our country; my side – your side, I'm right – you're wrong. There is a fundamental lack of respect and true communication that would lead to understanding. I think the root cause is discrimination: racism, sexism, and classism. A backlash from President Obama has led to a violent resurgence of racism, and our current President (Trump) has exacerbated everything, striking every nerve with a hammer."

The survey question elicited political observations from some of the respondents. Anita of Great Falls, MT, sees a definite breakdown in morality within the USA today. "The liberals and progressives removing God from all areas of society, the growing secular culture devolving life in all stages through rampant abortion and encouraging euthanasia are all components of the downfall. Other causes include pushing the homosexual agenda in schools, boy scouts, etc. Obama Care encourages abortion and discrimination against the elderly. The violence and profanity and sex glorified in movies, music video games and TV are all factors."

Nancy from Cleveland, OH is not so pessimistic. "I don't think there is a breakdown in the morality of the present day." The retired corporate attorney explained, "I think every generation or time period has some who are good and moral and some who are not."

"I don't know if there is a breakdown in morality," said Heather of Verona, WI. "It's always been there because of power and privilege and the institutions of racism and sexism and how it's played out that made it the norm. I think that makes us a less moral society."

Kathryn from Flanders, NJ, said, "Of course there is a breakdown in morality. The idea that we must not judge the attacks on religion – we have no moral path."

Gadgets and games contribute to the breakdown, according to Neva of Des Moines, WA. "Attention is taken away from family time and meals are no longer together as a unit."

How could family ties be strengthened and morality resurrected?

"Ban the X-Box," says Gloria from Wilmington, VT.

Phyllis from Fountain Valley, CA, attributes the breakdown in morality to "The media, internet and smart phones which have eroded the values of traditional families."

Jennifer of Scituate, RI, said, "I see a breakdown in empathy which is incorrectly labeled as a breakdown in morality. Too often people equate morality with religion. Empathy is universal. Things would be so much easier for everyone if we chose kindness over finger pointing."

Ashville, AL, resident, Elaine noted, "Too much divorce," she said. "Children are bounced between homes often, not always, I realize, grow up insecure. Also too little discipline in the home, where respect for authority should be taught. Too many people grow up having everything handed to them, so they expect to have it that way as adults. They become selfish, and expect to have luxuries now that their parents took years to accumulate. Many have the 'live and let live' attitude, which is an impossible philosophy to maintain. One person's actions affect others, because as someone once said, 'My rights end where your nose begins.'"

"I think there is a general lack of pride in America and a lack of investment back into the USA," said Sarah of Chester, NJ.

"I'm not sure that there is LESS morality, but perhaps a different type," said Tricia, Nashville, TN. "Our society doesn't support children and families as much as they should. There is too much focus and need for long-hour jobs."

Diane of Kingstown, RI, was mixed in her response. "Yes and no. I think some of the present-day politics are adding to the breakdown in morality. Each generation has to set a standard. I try to remember that what I believe may not be suitable for a younger or older generation of Americans."

The State of the Union
Comfort Level with the Country's Economy

"There can be no liberty unless there is economic liberty."
~ Margaret Thatcher

"We're living in a whole new social and economic order with a whole new set of problems and challenges. Old assumptions and old programs don't work in this new society and the more we try to stretch them to make them fit, the more we will be seen as running away from what is reality."
~ Ann Richards

The majority of women responded they were uneasy about the economic state of the country. While many directed their answers in a broad manner toward society in general, several of the women spoke only from the reference of how well their own town or state or for that matter their own finances were doing.

It came as no surprise that 66.8 percent of the sample population felt they were "very concerned" about where the nation is headed. Another 23.1 percent were "somewhat" worried regarding the stability of the economy; 6.87 percent thought things were "just fine," and 3.1 percent said ,"Do not know enough about the economy to make a comment."

Several had their own takes on why our economic crisis is happening and who or what is to blame. For most, politicians are the core of the problem.

According to Kelly from Slidell, LA, "We are in a crisis due to out of control government spending. Difficult decisions need to be made to get control of the situation."

"Who is running the show?" wonders Peaks Island, ME resident Rachel. "I think the government and the economy are generally run by a small percentage of people in top grossing industries. This is very uncomfortable to me."

Though political loyalty or affiliation was not overtly asked of any of the participants in the survey, frequently their subjective views of the current and past administration seeped into their comments.

"The economy was on the upswing," said Jennifer of Scituate, RI. "President Obama offered many a 'hand up' and they were able to lift themselves out of poverty. The current president is going to set us back."

Other women looked not to the oval office as the root of the economic woes but rather the lies coming from within Congress.

"The deadlock in Congress is troubling. They can't seem to get past posturing to find middle ground," said Nancy, Cleveland, OH. "But I see signs of improvement in housing, jobs and less dependence on foreign oil. So there's a more positive feeling than previously."

Rachel from Downing, MO, was more troubled. "Our economy is unstable as our nation's leaders engage in frivolous spending and have cuts in programs that cause loss of jobs and loss of resources."

Rebecca of West Plains, MO, goes even further. "I'm not comfortable and I foresee we are headed for bankruptcy like Greece."

Juliana of Double Star, WY, has dire concerns about the US economy. "We are due for another revolution. There is no confidence in the government and it's coming out of chaos."

And who is at fault?

That depends on who you ask and where they live.

Mila of Chester, NJ, said, "The Obama failed administration."

"Big government must take the blame for the economic status," claims Hackettstown, NJ, resident Lorraine. "*We the people* no longer hold power over the government, instead we have lost our – power to banks and corporate America – something that JFK warned us about years ago.

"Welfare is a way of keeping the poor – poor and not paying off on our own debts leaves us at the mercy of those we owe or committing evil acts to stave off their payback or interest."

High taxes, nuclear threats from abroad, terror attacks on US soil, the economy, the jobless rate, and poor healthcare are all issues facing Americans.

Roxanne of Roy, UT, said, "The economy is in bad shape. It's hard to find jobs and the taxes where I live are so high and it's hard to make ends meet."

Sometimes a solution to our economy can come from home. Calling the economy "scary," Nannette of Surprise, AZ said, "We as a country are so deeply in debt that our own great-grandchildren will still be paying for our ridiculous debt from today, I can't change that but I can hopefully teach my children to be responsible with their money, invest in their education and help them understand the difference between needs and wants so they don't overextend the way or government has."

Lydia, of Newark, DE, shared the educational aspects of living in a difficult economy. "There is a lack of education about money that is rampant in Congress and in our homes. People feel they are entitled to luxuries, instead of having to earn them. The federal government as an entity has lost touch with what's most important to its citizens."

The lack of good jobs struck a chord with some of the women who have personal experience in their own lives. And while the government can't seem to control the nation's finances, individuals and families, in some cases, are real victims.

"There are just no jobs out there," claims Stephanie from Ballantine, MT.

Alysia of San Pedro, CA, is the widowed mother of six children. "I am very concerned about the economy. My office manager and I went from minimum wage to commission only. My company is outsourcing work. It's so very difficult."

Even those women whose families were somewhat secure voiced concern for other Americans not so fortunate.

"No one is secure in this economy," said Lois of Fairplay, CO. "Just because you have a job this week, doesn't mean you will have one next week."

Elizabeth of Westbrook, CT, added, "I'm not happy with the disparity between the wealthy and the rest of the people. Too much greed way at the top."

Thelma from Great Falls, MT, rephrased the original question: "Is there really ANY comfort in the state of the US economy?"

Some women were hit in the face with the economics they face in daily life. Anita from Great Falls, MT, said, "I have zero confidence in the economy."

Kay notices the economic changes when she shops at the supermarket in Honolulu, HI. "The prices are always going up and I feel very helpless about that."

Others across the country made the same observations.

"Just go to the supermarket and watch the prices," said Saralynn of Dakota City, NE. "It's continually going up because of the economy and the salaries stay the same."

"The cost of living is out of control," said Norma of Chester, NJ.

And Pat from Arvada, CO, maintains that, "The state of the US economy is a mess. My brother has had two failed businesses and with Unions there are no jobs."

Some women were content with the economy as long as their families were in good financial shape. Cherry from Rosemont, MN, said, "As long as I work and put food on the table for my kids I'm not upset about the economy. I'm not selfish."

Vicky of Lewes, DE, said, "We are comfortable, though I fear for social security for the younger generation."

Spring, from Walls, MS said, "I'm just fine."

Annapolis, MD, resident Tania shared her opinion on the economy. "I don't take great comfort in the economy, but as a whole I'm happy our family can take care of themselves."

Finally, Jackie of Mine Hills, NJ, said, "I can't complain about the economy. I'm personally stable."

Some women perceived the part of the country they lived in was not really impacted regarding a shaky economy.

"People out here in Fargo, ND, don't talk about the economy," said Frances of Fargo. "It's booming here, so it's not an issue here."

Rheba of Cincinnati, OH, said, "The economy is doing alright. I was a child during the Great Depression and we had a happy life even then and think now we are gradually coming out of it."

Also positive about the economy was Amanda of Shamokin, PA. The mother of six said things will get better now that Trump's in office. "It just sucks how he's being degraded."

Another group of women were unsure and ignorant of the details of Obama Care.

"We know so little about Obama Care and how and if it will affect Medicare," noted Elaine from Ashville, AL. "I'm 66 so Medicare is very important to me. I'm also concerned about folks not having jobs. How are they going to eat? Pay rent? I'm concerned Congress seems more interested in preserving party politics than what's best for the American people. However, I'm not as concerned of my future because God has always taken care of me and I know he always will."

Bonnie of Caldwell, ID, was very nervous about the future of health care as part of the economic equation. "I can only afford so much and I pay... but I give more out to others who don't even try to help themselves. Disability benefits and social security needs to be overhauled."

Those with limited incomes worry over continuing benefits to those who don't work at all.

Linda of Plainfield, IN, said, "We shouldn't be forced to give to others. Too many people don't choose to work – lots of free stuff!"

Jill from Quincy, IL, works in the medical profession, yet she remains skeptical of health care options. She witnesses daily changes in the field. "I would say on a scale from 1 to 10 with 10 the most nervous, I would say 8. My biggest concern is the cost. Working in healthcare now I see the cost and mark up of simple tests. I have seen a change in the last 10 years and cannot even imagine what it will be 10 years from now."

Stacie from Garwood, NJ, says, "I feel it might get worse before the economy gets better."

Mary from Albuquerque, NM, said, "The rich get richer and the poor stay poor. And the middle class just struggles. I feel that the state of the US economy is struggling to salvage social security as well."

"We have a failing economy, spinning further and further out of control," said Christy from Edmond, OK. "We are going into more debt while politicians are too fat and comfy."

A recent college graduate from South Carolina expressed angst about the economy. "I'm paying so much for college, but a degree won't guarantee me a job. I know social security may not exist either by the time I retire."

Tight finances are what prompted Amanda and her boyfriend to move in with his sister. "We don't make enough," said the Rapid City, SD, resident.

Jennifer of Scituate, RI, commented on health care from the top. "There are very few voices advocating for women's' health in the White House."

Lynnetta, Spring Hills, TN, noted her "extreme discomfort" with the economy. "Most people live paycheck to paycheck and are deeply in debt without savings. I'm no financial guru, but that's a train wreck waiting to happen. Whatever they did to prop up the economy after 2008 collapse only put things off and perhaps escalated the inevitable failure."

Finally, looking at the economy as a sign of the times, Joyce of Wirtz, VA, said, "There is no comfort about the economy. Too much is happening – no jobs, no money. I believe the end of times is closer than ever. There is no encouraging news."

Not everyone paints a bleak picture.

Lesley from Basking Ridge, NJ, says, "Things are slowly getting better. Obama has done a great job even if the congress blocked much of his plans to help the middle and lower classes survive. We'll have to see what happens with Trump."

Margaret of Derry, NH, is also more optimistic. "It's been a medium to bad place, but I think the economy is recovering."

Gail of Chester, NJ, said, "Since the crash of 2007 the economy seems to have righted itself as it seems and is working well."

Thelma of Cary, NC, sees a reason for positivity in the economy. "We will return to economic strengths. And we do need to strengthen the middle class."

Women from Pennsylvania, New Hampshire, New Jersey, Ohio, North Dakota, and Wisconsin all felt in the presence of a recovery with the new commander in chief in office. Ten percent opted to not answer the question, saying they don't know enough about the economy to make a judgment and or they do not have an opinion on the subject.

Life Now Better, Worse, or Same as Growing Up

"When we were growing up, we were so poor that our heritage was the only thing we had. Mama would say, 'kids, pour more water in the soup. Better days are coming.'"
~ Ashley Judd

Are women better off, the same, or worse in today's culture?

"Absolutely worse," said Gail from Magnolia, DE. "My dad was a blue-collar worker and my mom was a stay-at-home mom. We had a much better quality of life than today. We had a nice home, all the modern conveniences and traveled on only one salary. Today, you can't make ends meet on two salaries."

Jeanine from Honolulu, HI, concurred. "It's definitely worse now because of where I live utilities are astronomical, and so many different ecological aspects like banning all plastic bags at grocery stores and paying for biodegradable ones."

While decades ago people used cash as the main source of payment for goods/services, the emergence of the credit card allows a gap in the time needed to pay. While credit cards have advantages, they can also have their disadvantages as well.

There were similar sentiments from Albuquerque, NM, where Mary said, "In some ways we are not better off economically, because when I was growing up we lived within our means – no credit cards just layaways."

For Jackie in Brownsville, PA, things are "worse than when I was growing up. My investments are down with no increase in sight. Gas and ALL products are increasing in price while employers hold back because they cannot make a profit or expand their businesses."

For Anna from Monsey, NY, things have become disastrous. "Things are far worse than when I was growing up. We were never wealthy, but my mother and I were able to make ends meet and people in general were helpful and not as cruel. The greed and corruption has grown out of proportion. The Internet has taken numerous categories of jobs."

Krystal of Dickinson, ND, said, "I feel poor. There are way too many people without jobs – the government over spends."

At the risk of sounding too nostalgic, Judy of Indian Lakes, SC, declares, "My family is worse off now than when I was a child. Luckily, my husband and I were not extravagant spenders and kept to a budget so we could at least be comfortable in our old age. I would not want to be a young person or a young family trying to get work in our country today. When I was a child, there were not the 'have to haves' or technologies with monthly payments that have become an everyday necessity and not a luxury today. We found ways of entertaining ourselves and playing games and talking to one another in person rather than this society of isolating with technical cellphones. Enough said."

Phyllis of Fountain Valley, CA, said, "Without a doubt we are slightly worse off today."

"Basically I thought we were poor when I was a child and so I did not want to buy clothes because I thought it was wasteful," said Kay of St. Mary's, PA. "Seemed there was enough for the boys in the family though, because they always had a new car and paid cash for it. I feel we did okay; all got to go to college and built our house with no loans. Brought up paying for everything, yet people now get houses and end up better off with freebies and loans that we didn't have."

"Without a doubt things are worse for us now," according to Roxanne of Roy, UT.

Many women had more than one answer. Roberta from Randolph, NJ said, "My family now is probably better off, but on the other hand, I don't recall feeling rich or poor as a child, but it seems each succeeding generation has greater opportunities than the previous one."

Answers varied on this topic, not only depending on where the respondent lived, but when they were growing up.

Patricia of Sandyston, NJ, said, "I was a child during the Depression, so I am FAR better off now."

Thelma from Cary, NC, was adamant that now is better. "It's much better. We struggled. I came from a broken home... Parents divorced when I was nine years old."

Bonnie from Caldwell, ID, said, "We are better off financially but the family isn't the same emotionally."

Education and more job opportunities were also a factor in the way respondents defined their level of status.

Christy of Edmond, OK, said, "We are better off because we both have great jobs."

Tricia, who is an assistant professor in Thornton-Wells, TN, said, "Things are about the same but with more time spent working."

Linda of Indianapolis, IN sees things from the way things were when she was a child and how it is at present. "When I was a child things were different. Different meaning there were not as many economic issues to deal with. When I was a child about 50 years ago, life was much simpler. Today you have a lot of self-interest politics and the mindset is 'what's in it for me?' I believe the government and politics have way too much involvement in our lives."

Nannette from Surprise, AZ, said, "We were lower middle class when I was growing up. I don't think we felt 'poor.' I remember that we went to yard sales, didn't eat out much and had to be careful with money. We also went on vacations that I still vividly remember. Today, we don't go on big vacations often, but we do go on a lot of mini-vacations when we can afford to. I do NOT use credit cards to pay for these or for anything else. We go out to eat more often than I did as a child, but try to eat at home as often as possible so we save money and eat healthier."

Lynnetta of Spring Hill, TN, notes, "I am far better off financially. "I grew up in a dysfunctional, impoverished home where alcohol and drugs were the priority for what limited resources we had. I learned how to budget and save money and worked my way through school to become a first-generation Bachelor's degree holder."

"The higher education of my husband and I make us much better off than the families we grew up in," stated Frances of Fargo, ND. "We've been able to pay off our mortgage!"

"Things are very much better off now for my family," said Caroline of Great Falls, MT. "We were very poor with uneducated parents. I got educated and made sure my family did, too."

"Though I grew up in a comfortable, middle-class family, I'm much better off today than as a child," said Elaine, Ashville, AL.

And then there were those who thought things were "about the same" and others who found a silver lining in what their families have been able to accomplish.

Good Health is Priceless

"Health is not a condition of matter, but of mind."
~ Mary Baker Eddy

The vast majority of survey respondents indicated valid concerns regarding the state of healthcare, confusion about how far reaching and long-lasting Obama Care might be, and the influence of immigrants taking jobs which offer health care they might lose.

Of course, those women with preexisting conditions voiced the most trepidation. "I'm really concerned as I have been diagnosed as a diabetic when I was 18 months old," said Stephanie of Hill, UT. "With the health care field constantly changing, I don't know what that will mean in the future."

Gloria from Wilmington, VT, expressed similar unease about the health care plan. "I worry because I have macular degeneration. What will that mean for me down the line?"

Joyce of Wirtz, VA, was disquieted about falling in and outside of her home. "It's so easy to trip and get hurt. I give a whopping level 10 for health worries. So many things are falling apart!"

Julianne of Double Star, WY, is coping with multiple sclerosis. "I have had this for 22 years and you're damn straight I'm worried about where healthcare is going."

Neva of Des Moines, WA, rates her concern as a 6/7. "We are retired military and presently have good healthcare BUT SLOWLY, slowly things are being taken away. What's next?"

"I think our system is terrible," said Anka from Avon, IN. The loan documentation specialist complained that, "The cost doesn't equal the quality. Other countries offer better options for less. I'm concerned I will have to pay more for fewer appointments and lesser care."

On the scale of 1 to 10 with one the least concerned and 10 the most, Rachel from Peaks Island, ME, chose a 10. "I believe in socialized medicine and single payer health care. I am very concerned about industry and business at the top grossing companies affecting me and the care of our citizens. Money at the expense of lives, that's what bothers me."

Having lived abroad, Sarah of Chester, NJ, is in a position to compare alternatives to care here in the USA. Yet she rated her anxiety at 10. "I lived with a national healthcare system in the UK. It has great aspects, but for serious FAST care it's terrible. My friends waited two days for a surgeon to look at his radiographs to see if surgery was necessary."

"Today's modern medicinal practices are reactionary, not preventative," noted Telia of Bowling Green, KY. "I've had family members die of lung cancer and colon cancer that never smoked and had maintained a healthier lifestyle than my own. Makes me believe more and more that regardless of how much effort you give to stay healthy, when your time's up, it's up point blank."

Bonnie of Caldwell, ID, claims she is "nervous" about health care. "I can only afford so much and I do pay... But I give more out to others who don't even try to help themselves. Disability, social security needs to be overhauled."

Many of the women bemoaned the high cost of paying for health insurance.

"We pay $3,600 a year for medical insurance," said Sheila of Tannersville, PA. "I am highly concerned about the future of the health care options and hope we can find something that costs less."

Some women who worked within the medical field observe the changes of care and voiced first-hand experiences and, thus, great concern.

Lauren of Okeechobee, FL, said, "I am diabetic with several health issues. I am very worried because I also do smoke."

Lois from Fairplay, CO, said, "I would score it a 10 on a worry scale. Insurance is just too expensive and right now we are unsure of the effects of Obama Ccare."

Although her own personal healthcare issues she rates as 3, Diane of Anchorage, AK, noted conditions for others, especially the elderly. "I live in a state where Medicare does not cover the cost of the average cost of a doctor's visit. Therefore, many healthcare providers have stopped accepting Medicare patients."

Pat from Arvada, CO, rates her concern about her health and health care options at the top of the list, giving it a 10. "It's mainly due to not knowing all there is out there. Obama Care needs clarifying and I don't want others deciding my fate. I raised three kids on my own and I want to make my own decisions.

Amanda from Rapid City, SD, works as a front desk supervisor at a major hotel chain.

The divorced mother of one she said, "I have no insurance now, it's just too expensive."

From the standpoint of the environment, Jennifer, who is the manager of the Ambassador Animal Programming at the Roger Williams Zoo, said, "I am worried that natural resources will be strained by climate change. We need to ensure access to clean water for all Americans while we reduce carbon."

Wanda, Memphis, MO is retired. "I keep thinking is there going to be any healthcare for our children and grandchildren?"

Tracey from Hackettstown, NJ, graded her level of anxiety about healthcare as a 10. "I'm tired of killing myself at a job for some of the work benefits and everyone thinks people should get it for free."

Vicky of Lewes, DE, also places her fears at the highest end of the spectrum. "I have had surgeries and lots of health issues. I don't know what will happen if insurances decide to deny coverage to those of us who have preexisting conditions."

"As a diabetic, I am really concerned about my health and health care options in the future," said Stephanie, Ballantine, MT.

Pamela of Flanders, NJ, is only moderately concerned about healthcare. "I do fear insurance will become more expensive than ever and harder to get. I also fear Medicare/social security will become a thing of the past."

Lisa of Plainfield, IN, is divorced and is alarmed to the max about her health. "I keep paying more per month, increased co-pays, increased deductibles and less service. I fear serious illnesses may not be treated properly."

"I rate my apprehension with a 7 out of 10," said Tricia of Nashville, TN. "Health costs are unpredictable and can be catastrophic, even for relatively common healthcare problems (for people in middle/older age)."

Alyssia of San Pedro, CA, feels she is in a difficult predicament. "I don't have any health insurance and rarely go to the doctor. I am the widowed mother of six children and keep hoping that because I am young enough, I can hold out till insurance becomes more affordable and available."

Politics continues to dismay and distress many of the women who responded to the survey.

"Mental health, physical infirmity and suffering are my concerns for myself and my family," said Kathy of Randolph, NJ.

There were some women who said they had no real concerns, as their health was good at the present.

Elizabeth of Westbrook CT, explained, "I am very healthy right now, so I don't give it much thought."

Concerns/Solutions for Yourself and Aging Family Members

"The best thing about being over 70 is being over 70. Certainly when I was 45, the idea of being 70 was like, 'Arghhh!' But you only have two options in life: Die young or get old. There is nothing else. The idea of dying when you're 25 is kind of cool – a bit romantic like James Dean. But then you realize life is too much fun to do that. It's fascinating and wonderful and emotional. So you just have to find a way of negotiating getting old psychologically and physically."
~ Helen Mirren, AARP Magazine, Dec. 2016/ January 2017.

In January 2016, The Population Reference Bureau report, "Aging in the United States," projected the number of Americans aged 65 and older will double from 46 million this year, to over 98 million by 2060. As a nation, we cannot overlook these figures. Healthcare, skilled long-term and short-term care, assisted living, rehab facilities, and an adequate number of professionals will be needed to cope with this demand.

Debilitating illnesses, nursing homes, and death were frequently mentioned by women who felt a degree of unease about their family's future.

"I watched my 58-year-old mother crumble when my dad died. I wonder, how would I ever be if that happened to me at that age?" posed Brie of Clayton, NC.

"My dad died about three years ago," said Jasmine of Dartmouth, MA. "His loss really took a toll on my mom. We moved in together after she sold my childhood home. She spent two years disconnecting and did very little day to day. She is 60 and I was scared that I would have to take care of her the rest of my life. I wasn't ready for that responsibility, and it was sad to feel that I lost both parents in a way."

Recently widowed Josephine of Fairfield, CA, said, "Now, I worry about myself."

Christy of Edmond, OK, stresses about the aging population in general being overlooked and forgotten. "My solution might be to assign mentors to every elderly person who does not have attentive family members to check on them and advocate for them. Perhaps high school or college students could be in some type of program."

Visiting a nursing home can be a difficult event.

Joan of Brockton, MA, said, "You wonder and worry how people are treating the elderly when relatives are not around to see what goes on after visiting time."

Phyllis from Fountain Valley, CA, said, "I'm afraid my mom will die soon and I am concerned that I will get cancer or some other debilitating conditions."

Anchorage, AK, resident Diane, said, "I'm worried about the lack of healthcare providers. One solution could be increasing the amount paid to cover the actual cost if you live in a high cost-state. Also, crack down on fraud."

Lynn of Wilmington, DE, said, "My greatest concern about aging is that I want to stay in my house all my life, as my mother did, and to be as self-sufficient as she was, still a safe driver at 93 and managing her own affairs until quick death from a heart attack. I worry about the possibility of a slow decline and being a burden. I hope to just keep going, eat well and exercise and deal with whatever comes my way."

"My concerns are what will be available for long-term care if I am ill and unable to care for myself," said Jackie of Brownsville, PA. "Currently Medicare can and does offer my parents enough benefits for long-term care and options for affordable healthcare. But when I age I do not see the same level of care or options available. My solution? Get rid of Obama Care. Reduce the number of entitlements or restructure benefits offered to nonworkers and people who are not US citizens."

Some women took an intergenerational approach to aging.

"I'm thankful that my parents are still pretty healthy," said Nannette from Surprise, AZ, "but I know that there may be a time when they need a lot of help. I've always known that I will be the one to take care of them, happily. I really don't know what they have done to prepare for future medical or independent living needs. I worry about that because I don't know how/if I will be able to help them much. I am already thinking of my next home as one that will be prepared for them also. I have had all this on my mind for a long time actually. One of the things that drive me to achieve what I have academically and vocationally is that my goal is to someday fully be there for my parents and my children/grandchildren."

Lisa from Stratford, CT, suggests "tax breaks for families with elderly members" as a potential solution to the issue of eldercare.

Several women feared a future in a nursing home.

Lorraine of Hackettstown, NJ, said, "I'm concerned about ending up in a nursing home. My solution would be to make home care more affordable so that anyone who wants can stay in their own home till the end."

Saving for the future isn't always the answer, some women said.

Gail from Magnolia, DE, noted, "My mom and dad did all the right things in saving for retirement and things beyond their control happened and at the end of their lives after working so hard, they ended up on Medicaid. I don't know what the solution is. Long-term health care is unaffordable. You just can't predict what your health costs will be."

Sara of Chester, NJ, said, "I'm afraid of health problems, leaving a legacy and having important ideas passed down and making sure I learn family history before people pass."

Staying positive and working on preventative strategies is another area mentioned in the survey.

Caryn of Roswell, GA, notes that "I lost my mother when I was 36 and she was just 66 years old. I try not to think about myself aging... I worry what will happen to me and my daughter, but I try to do what I can to prevent it – doctor regularly, eat better, exercise, etc."

The potential of no social security benefits was a concern of several women.

Linda of Plainfield, IN, said, "I worry about the lack of benefits and living in a nursing home and Alzheimer's! One possible solution is to privatize social security. Also, be very nice to your children and hope your health stays."

A Nationwide Survey conducted by the Harris Poll in 2016 indicated that women over 50 and older fear becoming an encumbrance to their families more than men. The Nationwide Retirement Institute polled 709 women and 582 men with 66 percent of the women saying they fear being a burden.

Healthy aging is the goal of all of the women.

"I'd like to keep mobile and healthy," said Marie of Bowling Green, KY. "My stress levels are already way too high for a 23-year old. I'll also like to keep maintaining our family farm and not sell out to neighborhood developers. I'm all for progress, but I'd also appreciate natural breathing space."

Kelly of Slidell, LA, is already caring for her aging mother. "Naturally I think about my own health as well. My main concern is not being able to care for myself and being a liability on my children. To that end, my personal solution is that I purchased long-term care insurance to ease any potential problems for my children."

Cherry from Rosemont, MN, says "I worry about my father. Mom died in her 50s of lung cancer and she never smoked. I worry about my children if I die." Cherry explains that she has no healthcare. "On a scale of 1 to 10 I would say my concern registers an 8. It's just too expensive, so though I am divorced my children are on their father's policy."

Anita of Great Falls, MT, said, "The effects of Obama Care could mean that at some point I will be denied care, even life-saving care. I would be forced to live a life of pain. That's chilling for me."

Staying in their homes as they age was an idea many women favored.

Trisha of Nashville, TN, said, "I worry about the lack of good, affordable options for in-home care and the costs associated with high quality care. I think insurance should be willing to fund more in-home care for extended periods of time as lower-cost alternative to institutionalized care. We need more nursing and physical therapy professionals as well."

Gloria of Wilmington, VT, said, "I *am* the aging grandparent and I fear for financial stability when it comes to aging health."

Joyce of Wirtz, VA, said her many ailments make her nervous and afraid. She has diabetes, a hernia, cornea transplants, back surgery, and knee issues. "I worry about not being independent and on my own. NO NURSING HOME for me."

While Neva of Des Moines, WA, claims she "has no health issues at present," but "the only solution to aging/healthcare is for GREED TO BE ABOLISHED."

Mental deterioration was mentioned, by many of the women in terms of their health as they age.

Heather of Verona, WI, said, "I fear the loss of the brain's thinking ability. My parents' whole idea of them relying on me instead of me on them. Not looking forward to that."

Tania of Annapolis, MD, is very fretful about health care in the United States. "My concern for my health would rate a '2,' but when it comes to healthcare options, I give it a '10.' Big PHARMA is a huge concern!"

The issue of aging comfortably when it comes to finance was mentioned frequently.

"It's totally a money issue for me," said Stephanie of Ballantine, MT.

"As a single parent of a handicapped daughter, my big concern is her future," said Thelma, of Great Falls, MT. "I'm sure my sons will provide for her, but not sure my step daughter-in-law will. She has always resented my daughter."

Anka of Avon, IN, believes, "Our system is terrible. The cost doesn't equal the quality. Other countries offer better options for less. I'm concerned that I will have to pay more for less care so I would rate it an 8."

"I worry about my current arthritis and asthma and possible future dementia," said Frances of Fargo, ND. "My parents are divorced and remarried and I find I am the sandwich generation: worried about my children and my parents at the same time."

Limited budget means limited care.

Lisa of Indiana is uncomfortable that she is alone. "I will have no one to care if I'm alive or dead. I also won't have enough money to have a decent existence. I need to make an effort to have connections with people and friends so it will be like family when I don't have any. For me, it's SAVE, SAVE, SAVE."

"I'm concerned with the high costs of nursing homes," said Barbara of Nazareth, PA. "I'm hoping we'll be able to afford it."

Distance not only can make the heart grow fonder, it can also present a source of anxiety when it comes to aging elders who live far from their children.

Janine of Honolulu, HI cited such a case. "It's hard to take care of my mother who does not want to live with me and lives so far away. In addition I have many questions of disabilities and mental situations."

Often, family deaths can impress a woman's reflections on her own health and mortality.

"For me it's less about aging and more about death," said Roberta of Randolph, NJ. "We've had a few deaths in the family that have thrown me for a loop and made me face my own mortality. I am becoming more and more frightened and the frequency of thinking about death is increasing. I am very worried and sad that my mother may die soon. She is the dearest thing on earth to me and I can't see a life without her. The biggest concern about my parents is that they are far away and I can't get to them quickly."

The younger the woman responding, the less concern expressed about aging.

Debbie of Arkadelphia, AR, said, "I haven't really given it much thought right now."

Linda of Clermont, FL was also not as distraught. "Not right now. It's nothing I can stop. When it is our time to go, it's our time."

Nicole of Pittsburgh, PA, shared mixed feelings about the topic. "My concern is will I have to take care of them? And who will take care of me?"

Some women said they do not fear the aging process.

"All my family are dead. I never think of age; never do," explained Kay of St. Mary's PA. "Only worry I had was when I had to have a rotator cuff fixed."

Heather of Verona, WI, said she fears the prospect of dementia. "I fear losing the ability to do things that I feel make me human and happy, like my vision. Losing the brain's thinking ability is frightening. In addition, the whole idea of my parents relying on me instead of me on them, I'm just not looking forward to it."

Janet of Winston-Salem, NC, explained, "I never expected to get to 55, so I'm not too worried. We have planned ahead for retirement and if we are disabled later our kids do not have to worry."

Judy of Indian Lakes, SC, said, "I am getting older and my body is breaking down a little, so I am concerned and have health worries. But I do not mind aging as the alternative is death. Ha! Just a little humor on a dark subject."

Thelma of Cary, NC, noted, "My parents have passed. I'm glad to be blessed to be 68. I no longer color my hair, but keep smiling and live life to the fullest. Also it's important to lend a helping hand to others."

Pat of Sandyston, NJ, insists, "I am a total optimist. I'm 87-years-old, just totaled my car – no injuries – take Plavix due to a possible IA years ago, and Lipitor as a precaution. I have bought an endless pool and try to swim an hour a day."

Rebecca of W. Plains, MO, notes she recently lost her 94-year-old father. "I hope to be independent as long as I can and take what life gives me."

Fight or Flight?

"I dream of giving birth to a child who will ask, 'mother, what was war?'"

~ Eve Merriam

As Americans, women have different takes on whether or not they would approve of their children going off to war. Those who have children in the military support their decision wholeheartedly, but not always without trepidation. The same is true when the women have had husbands or parents in the military.

Pride was the most noted emotion military moms declared.

Stephanie from Hill, UT, has a husband serving in Kuwait. "I am very sad, but also proud."

Brie of Clayton, NC, said, "I have a son in the Navy. It scares me because you never know what event could happen to send him into conflict, but I am very, very proud."

Cheryl of Bandera, TX, owns a dude ranch. "I sent my two sons and am very proud of them."

For some women, the military have become a part of their life.

Caroline of Great Falls, MT, has a son who is "a lifer. And the idea of him going off to the war scares the hell out of me. I make myself a better person and pray a lot. My son is on his fourth deployment right now."

Krystal of Dickinson, ND explains, "My daughter is in the Air Force. I do not wish her to go to war, but I am VERY proud of her."

Marie of Flanders, NJ, said her one son did serve five years in the Navy. "It was a non-combat situation in Korea and Japan."

"I was thankful and still am that I never had to send a child to war," said Rheba of Cincinnati, OH. "Both my husband and my brother served and I know it is a dangerous way of life."

Once a family has experienced the ravages of an ill or wounded veteran, it taints their perception of serving in the military.

Jackie of Brownsville, PA, said, "I wish that service staff would have better benefits and greater support while serving overseas. My brother was in Vietnam and had no support upon his return. He struggles today as well as those of his friends who served with him."

Thelma of Cary, NC, brought up another angle for discussion. "I have empathy for those who serve and their families, however it has given those who do join a great career. That's just another way to look at armed services."

Barbara of Nazareth, PA noted, "It's everyone's responsibility to serve our country."

Some women were not against joining the armed forces, just the combat part.

Frances of Fargo, ND was emphatic: "I am 100 percent against all wars. I believe in conscientious objection. Besides, there are other ways to serve the country beside physical combat."

Others were rigid on their stance: *not my child*. For some, the location of the combat zone was paramount. It's one thing to defend our country on our own soil from invasion, but quite another to protect another country on foreign soil.

Nannette of Surprise, AZ, said, "Personally I would not want them to go into the military because of the chance that they could go off to war. What parent wants to lose their child? My dad lost his cousin in Vietnam and it was devastating for the whole family. I am so thankful for the sacrifice others make for our freedom and I naively wish we didn't have to fight to keep it."

Rachel of Peaks Island, ME, was adamant in her response: "I can imagine few things worse."

Kelly, from Slidell, LA, said, "My children are grown and never considered joining any branch of military. I'm sure if I had to send them off to war, it would cause anxiety for me."

Roberta of Randolph, NJ, thinks, "My child would not survive."

Health issues were cited by some women as an objection to sending their children into the military and possibly war.

Stacey of Garwood, NJ, said "I have two daughters. One would not be allowed to serve due to her health. As to the other, I would prefer she NOT go into any military services."

Elaine, from Asheville, AL, shared the same sentiment. "My daughters are grown but I often think about my grandsons having to go off to war. The very thought scares me to death. Our government is too quick to jump into or cause conflict without considering the cost in human lives, not to mention world PR for the USA."

There are no good reasons to send our children off to war.

Heather of Verona, WI, said, "I would be absolutely opposed."

Though Jasmine of Dartmouth, MA, has no children her opinion on sending our young people to a war is strong. "I would be against it. They risk safety, possibly dying far from home for some nebulous cause that is likely fueled by oil prices or some other corrupt cause."

Jennifer of Scituate, RI, voiced real concern about the prospect of a war. "I find it terrifying. I am very much afraid that my children will inherit a war that should not have been started in the first place."

Judy of Indian Land, SC, also voiced her protest about wars. "We need to protect OUR country and I am tired of 'useless' wars (Vietnam, Gulf Wars) that accomplish nothing but killing our soldiers."

"It's a scary idea," noted Gail of Magnolia, DE. "We aren't even fighting today for our own freedom, but for freedom of others who are not appreciative of our help. I would support a child of mine in their choice to serve and be proud of them and pray for them every day."

Patriotism also was conveyed in some responses.

Diane of Anchorage, AK, said, "I would support my child's decision to go if I felt the war was justified, e.g. Afghanistan but not Iraq or Vietnam."

"If they wanted to be there, I would have a lot of pride for my children as long as it was for the safety of our country," said Bonnie of Caldwell, ID.

Edmond, OK, resident Christy commented that, "War seems to be an unavoidable necessity. I would not want to send my child BUT if this was their 'passion, duty or desire' I would support that decision."

Sara Lynn of Dakota City, NE, said, "Since my son is only 18 months old, it's too soon to tell how I would react."

Tricia of Nashville, TN hopes things in the future will improve. "I hope I never have to face that and that they would not volunteer to do that and that they will have other, better options."

Home Ownership

"Home is the nicest word there is."
~ Laura Ingalls Wilder

For generations, an integral part of the American dream has been to own a home. And now with more women in the workforce, that dream has in many ways become a reality. While the size and types of home preferences have changed due to many factors, the desire is still evidenced by women's responses to the survey.

An overwhelming 70 percent owned their own home, 26.87 percent were renters, and 3.1 percent lived with their parents.

Apparently, single women can decide to skip the spouse but still want a house. In fact, according to a Zillow report on consumer housing, in 2017, single women represent 17 percent of buyers in the real estate market. Further, an American Community Survey of one year based on US Census Bureau updates found that 35 percent of adults rent, while 65 percent own a single family home, townhouse, or condominium.

The profiles of owners is indeed diverse and based on various facts such as age, health, widowhood, divorce, and the absence or presence of children in the unit being rented or purchased. In some cases of single parenting – either by divorce or widowhood – childless union and empty nesters over 50 find smaller units, such as condos or townhouses, preferable choices. They offer socialization and freedom from such physical burdens as snow shoveling and watering the grass.

Natalie from Surprise, AZ, explained that she bought her first fixer-upper at 21 and used the equity to buy two more houses over the next 20 years. "So,

I've owned three houses. Then everything changed when my position at work was eliminated and I was forced to file for bankruptcy. Now, I am so blessed to live in a home my parents bought as an investment and allow me to rent. It was a win-win situation for everyone and has allowed me to get my family and credit back on our feet. While we fully consider this MY home, I will be thrilled to have my name on a mortgage again sometime in the next few years."

Wanda of Missouri noted, "Owning a home has always been a goal for me. Although we still have a mortgage, we are working hard to pay it off and looking forward to a time when that will happen. Mostly, though, home is a refuge for us – a place to come home and feel safe for our family. It's a place where we are one."

Anna of Monsey, NY, was more somber in her response. "I have never owned a home. I haven't even rented one. With my disability and unemployment I have struggled to pay for apartment rent. With the downturned economy a few years back, I lost my job and now live in a single room of a furnished house. There is nothing personal about it; no warm 'homey' touches. I have my books and a radio and that's as 'homey' as it gets for me. It's terrible for anyone to live like this. When I was young I too had dreams of a career, a husband and a home. It wasn't to be. My own home, no matter how small would have been a dream come true. At nearly 70, that's all over now. Those who have a home are blessed and I wish them well."

Home ownership isn't the same as having a home, observed, Barbara of Irvington, NJ. "My German immigrant parents left me their home when they passed. But it is a home that holds many terrible memories. A home is supposed to be warm and supporting filled with good times and love. My son, who was ridiculed by his grandparents all his life because he was illegitimate and many awful things happened here – he set the house on fire, went to jail; my mother always called him 'unwanted'… But I earn a minimum wage and the best part for me is that the house is paid off, so I just need to worry about taxes. But looking back, this house was never a home, just a house."

Hobbies

"If you are losing your leisure, look out! – It may be you are losing your soul."
~ *Virginia Woolf*

The kinds of hobbies women engage in are as varied as the women themselves.
These include:
Acting
Amusement parks
Art
Arthritis water aerobics
Arts and crafts
Attending Blue Grass festivals
Baking
Barbecues
Basketball
Basket weaving
Beekeeping
Bible study
Bocce ball
Bridge
Camping
Canning
Cards

Car racing
Carousel restoration
Church events
Clay pigeon shooting
Club membership
Coaching kids' sports
Coloring
Crocheting
Collecting antiques
Computer club
Cooking
Cribbage
Cross country biking
Cross country skiing
Crossword puzzles
Curling
Dancing
Date nights
Dining out
Dog walking
Downhill skiing
Drawing
Fishing
Folk dancing
Football
Food tastings
Four-wheeler riding
Gardening
Hiking
Historical research
Home improvement projects
Horseback riding
Horseshoes
Hunting
Jewelry making
Jump roping

Karaoke
Knitting
Martial arts
Meditation
Motorcycling
Movies
Needlepoint
Number puzzles
Painting
People
Pet therapy using my dog at homes
Photography
Pilates
Pottery
Playing different instruments
Quilting
Reading
Red Hat society events
Roller blading
Roller skating
Rummikub
Running
Scrabble playing
Scrapbooking
Sewing
Shanghai Push Rummy
Snowboarding
Snow machining
Spending time with kids
Swimming
Table tennis
Tai Chi
Tennis
Theater
Thrift store shopping
Tooling around in golf carts

Traveling
Video games
Visiting with friends/family
Volunteering
Walking
Walking stick making
Watching documented ghost stories
Water aerobics
White House tour guide
Wine making
Wine tasting
Word puzzles
Writing
Writing poetry with husband
Yoga

The great outdoors is a stimulus for many responders who like to "get up and go."

Elaine, Ashville, AL, likes trail riding, as well as reading and crocheting.

Cindy, of Goose Creek, SC, also loves to ride horses on the southern beaches "as often as I can."

Owning a pet is often an impetus to outdoor exercise and fun.

Lisa of Indianapolis, IN, enjoys walking her dog and hiking in the great outdoors. "I also enjoy doing crosswords and watching documented ghost shows!"

For Ellen of Mt. Arlington, NJ, "It's kayaking," while Eileen of Las Vegas, NV, "Loves to do martial arts."

Participating in the arts is also a favorite of women. "I get a real itch to paint," admits Nannette from Surprise, AZ. "When things are just going well in my life is when it happens. It's essentially a sign of health and balance for me. I start feeling creative and want to paint anything I can. That has meant my entire house painted over three years, and I continue on canvas. Once in a while my art used to be landscapes and still life, but it has become more abstract and geometric over the years. I don't want to try to mimic something, but create from my mind and use a variety of materials and textures. I give these as gifts and or décor in my home and offices."

Music has the same draw for Rebecca of West Plains, MO. "I love to learn new musical instruments. I just learned the banjo and I love to go to Bluegrass festivals. When I'm not strumming away, I garden and hike. For the past nine years I have also enjoyed cross-country biking."

Admittedly, "self-taught" accordion player Kay, of St. Mary's, PA, not only enjoys all music, "save for real hard rock," but also volunteers her talents at local senior homes.

Several women stated they are heeding the call to the stage in local theaters.

Pat, Sandyston, NJ, is also breaking into recording audiobooks, while Kathryn of Flanders, NJ, acts at a local women's theater in the state.

More in the fast lane is Lydia of Newark, DE, who along with her husband, races cars. "I must say we do much less since our kids came along."

For Wendy, Albany, OR, the arts have taken on a big part of her life. She is active in her town's restoration of their carousel. The one-time owner of a coffee shop now enjoys preserving the merry-go-round. "Albany was changing and we had to find a way to reinvent ourselves," she said:

"In 2002 the community of Albany, Oregon became interested in creating a hand-carved carousel similar to projects recently completed in Missoula, Montana and Salem, Oregon. As a matter of fact it was a visit to Missoula that brought the idea of a carousel to Albany. We opened our carving and painting studio to anyone from the age of fourteen and up regardless of skill or background and began the process of getting animals adopted, carved, and painted. This carousel will have 52 animals and, being a menagerie style unit, will have a variety of animals ranging from a seven foot plus tall giraffe, to dogs, cats, zebras, unicorns, dragons, and yes, even lions, tigers, and bears, (oh my just to name a few)! The animals will be situated on three rows where the outside (large animals) will be standers while the middle and inside row animals (medium and small sized respectively) will be jumpers. Each row will also have two replacement animals and we also have five seasonal animals planned, bringing our total to 63 animals.

"We also were fortunate to have a 1909 Denzel Carousel Corporation mechanism donated to our project. Our initial plan was to purchase a new mechanism that would hold 32 animals. However, Bill Denzel who is the great grandson of Gustav Denzel, the founder of Denzel Carousel Corporation, heard of our project and arranged for an antique mechanism to be donated to us. Our mechanism has taken over 10 years to restore to working order. The amazing thing about this endeavor is that whenever we've needed something, it's been provided for us. Somebody's aunt knows somebody's uncle who comes down to lend a hand."

Seasons often dictate the participation of specific sports. While many of us have not until recently been familiar with the sport of curling, Gail of Chester, NJ, has enjoyed a long relationship with the sport. Though the first known curling events were set in the 16th century on lakes and ponds in Scotland, the activity has flourished to own its own event at the winter Olympics as an officially recognized sport in 2006.

Crafts occupy a popular choice for many of the respondents.

Peggy of Dover, NJ, finds knitting and crocheting very relaxing. "Then I wondered what am I going to do with all of these baby blankets and afghans? I donate them to the needy."

There is a craft for everyone who has the desire to create a unique piece of art. For example, Lorraine of Hackettstown, NJ, makes walking sticks, while Jeanine of Honolulu, HI, does basket weaving.

Jan and her husband of Ridgway, PA, invest some of their free time making homemade wines. "It's educational and fun and delicious!" she said.

Tricia of Nashville, TN, enjoys not only "wine tasting, but food tastings as well."

November is usually deer hunting season in Memphis, MO. That's when Courtney of Downing, MO, steps out of her office job and joins her dad and uncles in the sport. "I just love it. I grew up with, it you know."

Name a card game, and Judy of Indian Land, SC, has played it. "I'm very active in my community and love to play cards. This includes: Bunko, Mexican Dominoes, cribbage, Shanghai Push Rummy, Rumikub and hearts."

Being on the road is the fun aspect of antiquing for Pam of Indianapolis, IN, who said, "I really love it."

And Alysia of San Pedro, CA, "can't get enough of amusement parks. We travel all over the area to find them. They are such fun for the whole family!"

We've all heard about people who have a bee in their bonnet, but how about bees in the backyard? That's the newest adventure for Jennifer of Scituate, RI, who has been doing vermicomposting (using earthworms to convert organic waste into fertilizer) for quite some time. "Now I'm on to beekeeping," she said.

Staying Social

"I am a big believer that you have to nourish relationships."
~ First Lady, Nancy Reagan (1981-1989)

Do married couples still have date nights? Does each partner in a relationship enjoy interests/hobbies outside the home? Do couples regularly do things together? What influence do tight finances, care for aging elders, children's activities, and overworking have on a relationship and having fun?

According to the 2016 *Chase Freedom Unlimited Card* survey of more than 1,000 American adults, 97 percent of us think that having fun is very important. But only 53 percent of Americans – and just 49 percent of women – report actually having it on a regular basis. In fact, 81 percent of people wish they had more fun every day. (*Glamour* magazine)

That's often easier said than done. Getting home late from a job, carpooling children to sports and activities, participation in religious services or activities, tending to senior relatives, and a tight budget can put a crimp in anyone's "fun" time.

Stanford University happiness expert Emma Seppala, an author, speaker and research scientist, said in the Chase study, "If we focus on boosting fun and happiness in our lives, even in little ways, research suggests we can end up more productive, charismatic, energetic, and innovative."

When young children leave the nest, it is often easier to find time/finances to go out and have fun, so says Phyllis, Fountain Valley, CA. "Now the children are grown we are definitely more socially active."

Caryn of Roswell, GA, has two young children. "I think we are still socially active. We have always been good about giving each other a night to ourselves to do what we would like and then we also spend time together."

Lisa from Flushing, NY, notes, "We are socially active, but in a limited fashion. Schedules and finances are the issue in the frequency."

For Jackie of Brownsville, PA, "We are socially active but as we get older have noticed we like being home more. I would like to have more time to do activities for recreation but due to economic issues with the current president (Obama) I have to change plans for my retirement age."

Lorie of Bangor, PA, said, "I always make time for fun. I work hard and make sure I treat myself whether I'm with a man or not."

Frances of Fargo, ND, said, "Before the kids we had more time together. Now we try to go out on a Saturday night 'date' but it doesn't work out *every* Saturday."

"We are fortunate in that area," said Mary of Albuquerque, NM. "My spouse and I are socially active and have many mutual couple friends as well as our own friends."

Other women found it hard to socialize for various reasons, especially the state of one partner's health.

Carlene of Great Falls, MT, notes, "I have commitments to him. He has a number of health issues and doesn't get out. His kids hate each other and me – no exaggeration!"

Rheba of Cincinnati, OH, claims they as a couple have never been social. "My husband has never been very socially active, so we don't have or do things with friends. I do many satisfying things on my own, but his preferences do limit me."

Sheila of Tannersville, PA, notes, "We are very active and involved in our gun club."

Amanda of Shamokin, PA, said "Sundays are designated days to go out because he shoots at a gun club. We are lucky because the grandparents take some of our six children for the day."

South Carolina is home to Judy, who lives in Indian Land community. "We are really active," the northern transplant said. "We are on a budget and do not take trips or vacations, but I do not miss it as I feel like we live in a Disneyland right there with all the many, many activities here."

Though Lyneta of Spring Hill, TN and her husband work a lot, "We have fun and rest time scheduled every week."

Others, like Christy of Edmond, OK, cite "tight finances" as a reason for not socializing as much as they would like to. Cherry of Rosemont, MN, agreed. "Money puts a real crimp in terms of socializing for us."

Eileen of Las Vegas, NV, said, "We have done nothing in two years. Money is just too tight."

Having children also changes the social picture, some women maintained.

Lydia of Newark, DE, explained. "I would not call us specially socially active. We enjoy having friends over, we belong to a community pool and spend lots of them there in the summer, but work and children have certainly changed how we socialize; not for the worse, just different."

Community and church events are one form of socializing some of the women cited as important in their lives and marriages.

"I live in a vibrant community where we share dinners and social times as families in our homes and on the beauty of the island," said Rachel, a single mom from Peaks Island, ME.

Lisa of Indianapolis, IN, said, "We are not socially active. We do not have a real legitimate reason. I believe, we need to change."

Gail of Chester, NJ, said, "We are socially active and contribute to various community endeavors – we produce a monthly six- to eight-page newsletter and I am on the board of our curling club."

For Nanette of Surprise, AZ, a social life is something new she is enjoying now. "I spent so many years doing so many things that I 'had to do,' like work, home, kids, school. This was not bad, but I didn't have much of a life outside that. I think I forgot how to just have fun and relax. I am thankful my fiancé has helped me enjoy the art of fun. This has included going to theme parts with our kids, comedy clubs, picnics and outings with the Christian Motorcycle Association."

When two adults in a relationship both work, it can take a toll on fun time.

Rachel of Downing, MO, said, "We are moderately active, but our jobs involve long hours including paperwork on our off time. So though we do socialize, at church, we also are at a stage where we are quite comfortable staying and enjoying our home and each other."

Travel

"Human beings are more alike than unalike, and what is true anywhere is true everywhere, yet I encourage travel to as many destinations as possible for the sake of education as well as pleasure."

~ Maya Angelou

While statistics are limited, an estimated 32 million single American women traveled at least once in the last year and about three in 10 make treks five times or more, according to the Travel Industry Association. And an increasing portion of solo female travelers are the Baby Boomers and single mothers.

According to Market Researcher Yesawich, Pepperdine, Brown, and Russell, 87 percent of women say they go for the beautiful scenery, compared with 72 percent of men. The vast majority of women in the survey had not lived outside the US.

In a *Trip Advisor* survey that polled 181 women in Australia, the UK, the USA, France, Italy, Germany, Spain, Russia, and Southeast Asia, 41 percent said they've traveled alone before. But that figure spikes to 74 percent when combined with the segment of women who plan to travel solo in 2015.

How do the women in this survey rate? The majority – 41.6 percent – ranked themselves as "occasional" travelers. Many said they would love to travel, but don't for various reasons including children, finances, work commitments, family situations or care giving, or health issues.

Of those who do travel "frequently," 11.5 percent have covered the globe.

Anka of Avon, IN, said "I've been to 11 countries, but never France. That is where I would like to go."

Betty from Pennsylvania has traveled to Italy and Vietnam. "I'm always up for a good trip," she says.

Another 32.6 percent said they "rarely" travel, while 14.1 percent admitted they had "never" traveled, either within the USA or abroad.

Spending time abroad as a school experience, being born in another country, or living abroad due to military service in the family were other aspects of women's cultural experiences outside of the USA.

Mila from Chester, NJ, explained, "I was born in the Philippines, migrated to the US in 1968 legally and became a US citizen. I married in 1972."

Some, like Roberta from Randolph, NJ, worked and lived abroad as a nanny. "I wanted to learn languages and wanted to live in a different country to experience life in a different culture," she said. "So I spent six months in Holland and six months in France as a nanny."

Cherry from Rosemont, MN, was also born in the Philippines, and Linda from NYC, was born in Canada but moved to the US at an early age. "I moved back to Vancouver for two years and Montreal for two years. Having a different cultural perspective from north of the border often helps in understanding how Americans think. I spent six weeks in France for an art course and two months in London for work. Would love to work abroad if possible. I have never felt totally comfortable in the US."

And Liz of Westbrook, CT, lived in Mexico for four years, adding, "I wanted to experience a culture other than my own."

Jasmine, Dartmouth, MA, spent a semester in Ecuador studying tropical ecology and said, "I look forward to someday visiting the Florida Keys."

Pat from Arvada, CO, lived in Germany for a summer while Thelma from Great Falls, MT, resided in England for two years with the military in my family. "I got to visit France, Canada and Mexico."

Lisa H. from Indianapolis, IN, lived in Florence, Italy, for five months during her junior year of college.

Rachel of Peaks Island, ME, and Margaret of Derry, NH, studied abroad in Mexico.

Joan of Califon, NJ, lived in Germany for three years, while Sarah from Chester, NJ, lived in Edinborough, Scotland for four years attending veterinary school.

Nannette from Surprise, AZ, was born in Japan while her father was serving in Vietnam, and Bonnie of Caldwell, ID, also lived in Japan while her son was stationed in Okinawa.

Pat from Sandyston, NJ, said that because her father was a travel writer, they lived abroad. "From age four to five we were in England, from six to seven in France."

Because her daughter has an international job, Vicky of Lewes, DE, has visited "places like Cairo, Morocco, Japan, all over."

Whether a bona fide traveler or a novice, all the women described their "ideal" vacation should be dictated by having the necessary finances and time to go.

Gail of Magnolia, DE, explained, "I would journey back to Israel. I felt such peace there. I long to go back and take that journey back through Bible history."

Rachel of Peaks Island, ME, said, "I would love to spend a year traveling with my son around the world. We would live and study different cultures."

Rebecca of West Plains, MO, who "rarely" travels, dreams of visiting "the castles of Italy."

Some of the women were very altruistic in their ideal vacation ideas.

Spring from Walls, MS, said, "I would love to take a trip to an underdeveloped country and help the children there."

The romance of the past is what lures other women to their "ideal" vacation dreams.

Marie from Bowling Green, KY, would love to "go somewhere my old classic TV cowboys lived like Dodge City, KS, or Nevada. I love my Marshall Dillon and Little Joe Cartwright."

Trying new things was on the list of some of the women.

Lisa from Indianapolis, IN, said, "Ideally, I would vacation at least two weeks somewhere visually beautiful at the mountains or the sea. I would eat foods I never ate, do things I have never done and immerse myself in the culture of the area."

For Diane of Anchorage, AK, an ideal trip would be "taking the Orient Express from Paris to Istanbul."

Heather of Verona, WI, said she would love to "go to Sussex, England where my favorite artist – Cicely Mary Barder – was born. I would look at her work and garden and browse antique shops."

Some respondents chose to stay closer to home.

Lisa of Stratford, CT, was one such woman. "Give me an RV and I'll set out on the road to visit the USA."

Though Jennifer of Scituate, RI, rarely travels, she insists, "I would love to. I would love to go to New Orleans for the food, music and spooky things. And my ideal vacation would be a beach in Fiji with my family – and a nanny."

What cities do women want to visit? New York City, Boston, San Francisco, and Seattle took top honors from women in the survey.

Reading

"Until I feared I would lose it, I never loved to read. One does not love breathing."

~ Harper Lee

According to a new report from the National Endowment for the Arts, women continue to read circles around men, especially in fiction and literature with 64 percent of women reading at least one book in 2012 and 56 percent of those at least one literary book, compared to 45 percent of men with only 37 percent read at least one literary book.

Yet few of the women who responded to the survey fit into this mold. Even fewer are members of a book club. Only 26.2 percent of the women identified themselves as "avid" readers while a whopping 46.8 percent chose their label as "occasional" readers of a combination of novels, nonfiction, magazines, and research or professional journals. In addition, 23 percent of the women said they "never read" at all. Citing health issues and time commitments, another 2.5 percent said they "only listen to books on tape." Of all of the readers only 5 percent belong to a book club, and in some cases, those book clubs are of a special type of reading such as classics or religious materials.

Avid reader Kathryn of Flanders, NJ, said, "I belong to a classics book club and I love sharing their insights and points of view. Beyond that I read several books a month on my own."

Mila of Chester, NJ, said "I belong to a religious book club. There is friendship there with people who have a high moral character."

Judy of Indian Land, SC, explains that, "I used to be in a couple of book clubs when I lived up north, but since living in the south I am currently way too busy to join one now, though I did enjoy myself when I did belong."

Bonnie of Caldwell, ID, said she belongs to a book club. "I read books I would never think of reading and I am loving it. I also cherish my time with the others with different opinions."

Frances from Fargo, ND, said she is an avid reader and wants to start her own book club.

Rheba of Cincinnati, OH, describes herself as "somewhere in between avid and occasional. But I always have a book or magazine going. I read the daily paper and I belonged in the past to several book clubs. Now I'm down to one but it's been a great way of staying on top of books and finding new friends."

Nancy, from Cleveland, OH, agreed. "Book clubs are a great way to get together with friends and find books I might not have otherwise chosen myself."

"Occasionally, I read a lot many years ago," said Kay of St. Mary's, PA. "Then because of commitments with my father and a mentally challenged brother I had to back out. My solution? I avidly listen to audio books on tape in the car."

Linda of NYC commented, "Depending on time, work, or other distractions sometimes I read a bit every day, sometimes not for weeks at a time. I am trying to get into the habit of reading a bit before going to sleep and on weekends. I alternate fiction with research and daily read *The New York Times*. I have often considered joining a book club for the social interaction, but haven't done so yet."

Though she would love to read more, Leah, El Paso, TX, reads "when I can."

Lesley of Flanders, NJ, claims she is "an avid reader. I belong to a book club and have read books I would not have chosen to read and in most cases I have really enjoyed them. It was a new experience."

Rebecca of West Plains, MO, calls herself an avid reader. "I love to read magazines or the Bible. I'm also interested in early American history especially about things like the Pony Express."

Other women were not so prolific with their readings.

Elaine from Asheville, AL, says she never reads books and doesn't belong to any book clubs.

Alyssia from San Pedro, CA, said she loves to read, "especially books by James Patterson," but doesn't have the time at the moment, instead occupied with taking care of her six children.

Jill from Quincy, IL, also claims she "never reads books."

Ana from Monsey, NY, said she loves to read. "I'm always reading. I favor books about religion and history."

Liz from Florida admitted, "I used to read, but not anymore."

Tricia from Nashville, TN, explained, "I never read books, mostly science papers for work."

Bonnie from Caldwell, ID, belongs to an ESO book club. "Reading books I would never think of reading and loving it. I also cherish my time with others who have different views."

Jennifer of Scituate, RI, classified herself as an "occasional reader" who "aspires to be an avid reader."

What's for Dinner?

"Now, nobody can ever cook as good as your mama."
~ Paula Deen

We've all heard the saying, "you are what you eat" when it comes to food as real nourishment. Yet it can also be said that where one calls home may also dictate what one cooks in the kitchen and is served in local restaurants. It is not surprising then that southern women prepare gumbo, western cooks favor chili, and New Englander's love their chowder.

Each region of the country creates and perpetuates their unique cuisine. Rocky Mountain oysters and broiled salmon are indigenous to western cooking. The influence of Alice Waters is evident in fare served in California. Tables across the south offer pan-fried chicken, field peas, collard greens, turnip greens, cornbread or corn pone washed down with generous jugs of sweet tea.

No matter the locale the respondents all agreed that families who dine together are stronger. The typical family meal of the 50s and 60s has in many instances been laid to the wayside in favor of longer work commutes, children's sports practices, social activities, and single as well as two-parent households. As a result, many of the women acknowledged they eat out more often.

When they do stay home, the family favorites involving home cooked meals are widely varied. As one might suspect, the region of their home impacts on food selections, and the way that meal is prepared sometimes is passed down from generations, resulting in one of a kind, lovingly made handmade recipes.

Yet in the planned menus of many of the women, one dish was honored as blue ribbon with their families: Spaghetti and meatballs, followed closely by lasagna. Another frequently mentioned dish was pot roast with noodles.

Healthy dishes were also noted as popular in some families. Some, like Margie of Randolph, NJ, gets requests for "chicken stir fry with broccoli."

Patricia from Sandyston, NJ, claims, "I live very simply. I broil a piece of meat or chicken or fish, steam some green vegetable and eat huge salads and lots of fruit."

Linda, who lives in NYC and rarely dines out, says, "Our meals vary with the seasons. Salads are a favorite in summer, and hearty food like homemade soup, lasagna in winter with apple pie and ice cream a year-round favorite."

For Thelma of Cary, NC, cooking is enjoyable. My family's favorite dish is baked chicken with gravy and mac and cheese."

Steaks with grilled mushrooms and onions with corn on the cob gets a thumb's up at the table at Krystal's home in Dickinson, ND.

Ethnicity plays a big role in Anka's Avon, IN, kitchen. "All Yugoslavian food," she said.

Eileen from Las Vegas, NV, claimed her family loves her "green chili enchiladas, for sure."

Margaret from Derry, NH, says her family's favorite meal is, "Chicken paprikash."

Another New Englander, Gloria from Wilmington, VT, noted, "I love to 'build' a soup and make homemade bread to go with it."

"Brisket and mashed potatoes" hits a home run at the home of Joyce, Wirtz, VA.

Heather of Verona, WI, does a variation on traditional lasagna: vegetarian lasagna roll ups, which her family loves.

"Tempura of any kind" makes a home run in the family of Juliana of Double Star, WY.

For many of us, a meal is not finished without dessert, and for some, dessert can be a meal in itself!

Rebecca of West Plains, MO, is one such fan. "I love to make lemon meringue pies and everyone else loves it when I do!" she said. "It may not be a meal, but it sure tastes like one!"

Vicky of Lewes, DE, and Cherry of Rosemont, MN, were proud to say, "I don't cook at all." Vicky added, "My husband has always done the cooking and that's fine with me."

To Market, to Market

"The odds of going to the store for a loaf of bread and coming out with only a loaf of bread are three billion to one."
~ Erma Bombeck

A study in the April 30, 2013, issue of *Progressive Grocer* entitled "Women Dominate Grocery Shopping" revealed that although women represent a stronger force in the workplace their role in food shopping has remained fairly consistent: they are the primary shoppers for the family. The study, commissioned by the Private Label Manufacturers Association (PLMA) and conducted by global market researcher GfK Custom Research, North America, indicated that two-thirds of women still handle most of the grocery shopping. Of those women, three-quarters keep shopping lists and 53 percent take time to clip coupons and research sales. In addition, six in 10 women surveyed spend more than an hour in the supermarket.

Grocery shopping today offers a lot of alternatives. There are the big chain markets, farmer's markets for fresh produce, and high-end exclusive upscale markets offering a variety of ethnic cuisines and exotic produce. Women check weekly ads for sales and in some instances are extreme couponers.

Couponing has become a popular pastime in the past few years as a way to become smarter about saving. Coupons reduces the final bill and for some women, known as "extreme couponers," it's a matter of pride to help the family save money.

The state of the economy is a chief reason for this outlet. Nowadays, not only do women cut coupons from magazines but also search online for coupons to print out and get special deals for rock-bottom deals. Many women will buy multiple copies of local newspapers just for the coupon inserts in hopes of saving 90 percent on their shopping bills.

Many women see it as a game as well. The TLC Network's show *Extreme Couponing*, features savvy shoppers who can buy $500 worth of groceries for $25. It is, without a doubt, a time-consuming endeavor perhaps equivalent to a part time or full-time job outside the home.

Mobile couponing has also become popular, as smart phones increase in popularity. This allows consumers to download coupons onto their cellphones and show their phone screen to the cashier at checkout to get the discount.

One such couponer is Nannette from Surprise, AZ. "I am a price-match guru when it comes to shopping. I'll collect the week's ads from various stores and lay them all out. I start with the ones that are usually cheapest and circle the things I need that are on sale. Once I've gone through them all, I mark their initials next to the ad and take a picture with my phone. This is my shopping list (mostly). When I get to the Wal-Mart, I am very organized about the process, ringing up all the non-ad matched items first. I can easily refer to my phone but also lay the ad down and the items on top of it as the cashier often needs to see the actual and I usually know where my items are before they can find them in their ad copies. Sometimes people behind me get irritated. I am very efficient, so it goes fast but, sometimes the cashier can't figure out how to convert something and some people are just rude... unfortunately. Still, I save a lot of money for my family and am proud of that."

According to *Statista*, in 2016, there were 38,441 supermarket stores in the country offering natural and/or gourmet foods. These include, but are not limited to, such major chain stores as ShopRite, Weiss, Acme, Stop & Shop; Carrs, Jewel-Osco, Lucy, Pavilions, Randalls and Tom-Thumb, Safeway Inc., Shaw's and Star Market, United Supermarkets, Food Lion which is a brand under Ahold Delhaize, Hannaford Giant Carlisle; Kroger, Dillons Supermarkets, and many more.

Linda of Indiana said she will buy a store name brand if it is less expensive than national brand names when she shops at Kroger and Wal-Mart.

Nancy of Cleveland, OH, explained, "We shop at a midsized regional grocery chain because we like their selection and their produce. We don't need huge quantities found at the big box sores. We do use coupons but not in the extreme."

Big stores like Wal-Mart operate 3,522 stores plus 699 Neighborhood markets and 660 Sam's Clubs while Trader Joe's has 467 stores. Whole Food has 430 stores as of June 14, 2016.

Some of the women are admittedly "picky shoppers."

Elaine of Ashville, AL, noted, "I don't go to a store based on sales or flyers, but might take advantage of a sale once I'm there. And I NEVER shop at Wal-Mart or Sam's!!!"

Markets like Costco Wholesale attract the likes of Diane from Anchorage, AK, while Alysia of San Pedro, CA, shops at "regular stores for my six kids and occasionally at places like Trader Joe's."

For Jill of Quincy, IL, "I go to Aldi's a lot. Its very cheap and saves us a lot of money."

Several of the women like Phyllis of Fountain Valley, CA, and Caryn of Roswell, GA, said they shop at not only chain stores but also at Costco Wholesale. Such stores promote their quality, brand name merchandise at substantially lower prices than are typically found at conventional wholesale or retail sources.

"Nothing can beat farm fresh" is the motto of some of the respondents to the survey. It is not a surprising comment coming from respondents in the Midwest where acreage is aplenty and farming is a way of life. This includes Lisa, Indianapolis, IN, who "prefers going to farmer's markets or specialty health food stores to supplement my diet."

Taking advantage of fresh local produce is a regular shopping choice.

Joanne of Milton, IA, frequents the Amish store near her. "I don't get everything there, but they have good deals on large quantities of potatoes, onions and vegetables."

Celeste also of Iowa, grows corn and soy on her farm. "Can't beat home grown."

Similarly, Rachel of Peak's Island, ME, shops "a combination of locally owned produce markets, Farm Share and growing our own food as well as Whole Foods."

Sometimes, when you can't grow it, you join others who can. Such is the case for Frances of Fargo, ND. "We belong to a local food coop. It's really cheap and organic."

"It's organic all the way," according to some of the shoppers in the survey.

Kristy of Edmund, OK, said, "We shop at Trader's Joes, Sprout, Whole Foods and organic is the way we go."

Finally, a few of the women like Stephanie, Hill, UT, explained her family's shopping routine, "My husband is in the military and their commissary is our source of food purchase."

Watching TV

> *"Reagan didn't socialize with the press. He spent his evenings with Nancy, watching TV with dinner trays. But he knew that to transcend, you can't condescend."*
>
> ~ Maureen Dowd

Depending on where you live, it's referred to as "the boob tube," the "telly," "the idiot box," "the one-eyed monster," or the "electronic babysitter." It's most common terminology is the television.

The typical American spends four hours and 51 minutes in front of a TV screen per day, according to a report from ratings company, Nielson. That research showed women watch television almost 40 minutes more each day than men; however, men spend 48 minutes a day using a gaming console on the TV compared to 22 minutes for women.

The Bureau of Labor Statistics conducts a "time use" survey every year that shows how typical citizens portion their activities thorough an average 24-hour period. The latest report covering 2013 found that 80 percent of us watch TV on any single day and that television took up more than half of all our leisure time.

In addition, the survey shows that men watch TV more than women, and TV time grows as you age. Americans in their retirement years spend twice as much time per day watching TV as young people do.

Nielsen's data show that Americans are busy shifting their viewing from broadcast TV to on demand, streaming video services. Live TV viewing is down 12 percent so far this year, according to a *Wall Street Journal* estimate, which explains why ratings have been falling for major networks such as Disney's ABC and Discovery's *Animal Planet*.

The majority of women, 51.8 percent, classified themselves as "somewhat interested"; while an additional 18.5 percent said they were genuinely interested (very important to important) in watching television regularly. Those watching "very little" television amounted to 19.9 percent, with another 4.3 percent noting they "never watch" TV. An additional 6.1 percent did not respond to the question.

Many of the women cited tuning in to the television to create background noise as they did their work or household routines. Those with young children were not embarrassed about using it as a babysitting device. Others who lived in the country with little access to social events also utilized television as a companion.

Among the very important television watchers is Jan of Ridgway, PA, who said, watching "TV is very important. But, I'm not really content with that answer."

Amanda of Shamokin, PA, is the mother of six young children. "My TV consists of cartoons all the time, and for now I'm okay with that."

Sherry of Rosemont, MT, agreed. "It's basically a babysitter for me."

"Television is my relaxation and I am okay with that," said Brie of Clayton, NC.

Background noise is how many women who have the television on constantly described their habits. Some explained it's like having a live person there with you, even though you are alone.

Liz, Goose Creek, SC, remarked, "It's very important to me as it keeps me company."

Other family members interests often dictate how much television is watched or in the background.

Heather of Verona, WI, said, "TV watching is extremely important to my husband but not at all to me. The kids are somewhat in between and no I'm not happy with my answer."

According to Elizabeth of Beckley, WV, "TV is too important here."

When you stand on your feet all day at work, sitting and watching a favorite program is an easy habit to fall into. It's looked upon as a reward to oneself. That's what Tracey of Hackettstown, NJ explained in her answer. "We live by the TV," she said. "I would like to get away from it, but I'm lazy. It's just an easy thing to do after a long day's work on my feet."

Kelly of Slidell, LA, was similarly dismayed with her family's preoccupation with the television. "They watch too much TV. I wish we could cut down on the amount we watch."

For Wilmington, VT, resident Gloria, "TV is more important to those who live with me (daughter and two grandkids, 13 and 14)."

Lacking social activity, the television can become a welcome presence in the home.

Jeanine from Honolulu, HI, said, "Television is very important to me since I'm a widow and am not into bar hopping. It is my outlet."

Staying current on local and national news was cited by Norma of Chester, NJ, as a reason for frequent viewing. "TV is very important as it gives us a window into information on world events, nature, science, arts and place of interest that I might not otherwise have access to."

Then there are the women who assume the label of "occasional viewers."

"Television viewing in our home is used for the news, Masterpiece Theater and Netflix," said Mary of Albuquerque, NM. "That is it."

Only a small number of respondents have "sworn off" television. It's a trend for some families since the 1994 grassroots event known as "TV Turn-Off week" was endorsed by over 65 national organizations including the American Medical Association, the American Academy of Pediatrics and the National Education Association. The event was slated in reaction to the concerns about the health, social, and educational impact television was having on young people.

During this period, kids and families pledged to turn off their TV for the week and find out the wide range of possibilities open to them when the television is not a part of their lives. The week-long abstinence from television was fostered by the concern of the passive sedentary nature of sitting and watching programs as well as the addictiveness of hours of viewing at the detriment of more physical and mental activities.

Only 6.1 percent of the respondents to the survey aired their criticism of the venue and have gone cold turkey from watching TV. Violence, overt sexual acts, and crime and drug portrayals were some of the areas viewers object to in their daily viewings.

In addition to these objectionable presentations, some women wrote about the obvious negative treatment of women broadcast on popular TV shows, giving such behavior an okay stereotype.

"Growing up we rarely had a TV and when we did my siblings and I were only allowed one hour of TV per week," said Roberta of Randolph, NJ. "I am the youngest and I had to watch what my two older brothers wanted to watch. We also were not allowed to watch gun shows – no violence or Superman (sacrilegious – nothing more powerful than God). Every Saturday night we all watched Jackie Gleason together (when domestic violence was acceptable!!! Even as a five-year old I thought how he talked to Alice was despicable. I knew I'd NEVER allow anyone to treat me that way)."

Juliana of Double Star, WY, explained, "TV has no importance for me."

Lyneta of Spring Hill, TN, does not miss television. "We haven't had a TV for 16 years and wouldn't have it any other way. We do enjoy a movie night then and again, and often see movies in the theater."

Linda of NYC is a proponent of no TV. "I haven't owned a TV in seven years and have no intention of buying one again. We enjoy watching a TV show on the laptop computer on Hulu or PBS occasionally while we have dinner and another late sitting in bed before sleep. We get to choose what we want to watch and when without annoying commercials or announcements of what is coming up at the 11 p.m. news. I used to joke that daytime television was invented to keep people at work. Now I wonder if all television programs are part of a government plot to communicate to alien life forms that might be listening in that there is no intelligent life on earth."

No one in Amanda's Rapid City, SD, home has interest in viewing the program on television. "We don't watch TV **at all**."

Jennifer of Scituate, RI, said, "To me TV is not at all important. To my family it is very important and I hate that."

Pets

"I never met an animal I didn't like."

~ Doris Day

We love our pets. In fact, many of us find them more gentle, respectful, and accepting than our fellow humans. We pamper them and treat them to the best medical care we can afford. And to prove our love for our animals the American Pet Products Association (APPA), total pet industry expenditures reached $60.59 billion in 2015. That's up from $58.04 billion in 2014.

A May 2011 Harris Poll found that 69 percent of women are much more likely to own a pet than men (55 percent). The difference grows greater when one considers which generation of women own more pets. Generation X, the survey states, ages 35-46, are the most likely to own a pet at 70 percent while Baby Boomers (66 and older) are least likely at 46 percent in the poll.

Regionally speaking, the poll found that those residing in the midwestern states accounted for 54 percent of owners, while easterners made up 61 percent. Southerners ranked at the top of the poll with a 65 percent tally, while westerners also came in at 65 percent.

In addition, pet ownership seems to drop with education, as 64 percent of those with a high school diploma or less or some college own pets compared to 59 percent of college graduates and 56 percent of post graduates.

But what did our women in the survey think?

The split between the haves (own a pet) and the have nots (don't own a pet) was pretty evenly divided with no apparent predilections of ownership related to geographic location. Women who owned a pet represented 47.5 percent while those who do not represented 48.1 percent. The remaining 4.4 percent did not answer the question.

When it comes to the big question: dogs or cats? A 2006 Gallup poll says that by a 7 percent to 20 percent margin, Americans describe themselves as a dog person rather than a cat person. But no matter the pet or breed, pet owners are enthusiastic about their animals.

Barbara from Chester. NJ, used to rescue Bichon Frise dogs. Now she has three dogs, one bird, and nine outdoor cats. "They all bring their own personality and make our family's life a lot of fun."

Marcella of Randolph, NJ, not only loves her three dogs but shares one of them as well. "I have a Golden Retriever, an Italian greyhound and a mixed breed. They bring love, companionship and loyalty to my life. I am an animal rescuer and regularly do volunteer work with my certified therapy dog, Boomer, a retriever. In retirement homes the people have come to love her so much they eagerly look forward to our visits. The same is true when we visit schools."

The more traditional dog or cat pets now share homes with other types of animals including rabbits, gerbils, chickens, goats, horses, and llamas.

Phyllis of Fountain Valley, CA, said, "We have a rabbit and two guinea pigs. They have brought a huge mess to clean up into our lives."

Vicky of Lewes, DE, is a true cat lover. "It's become a hobby, really," she said.

Sherry of West Orange, NJ, calls her dog "the daughter I never had."

Emotions run high amongst pet owners.

Kay of St. Mary's, PA, "used to have a horse, a dog and a cat. That was the best time of my life."

For Gloria of Wilmington, VT, "My wonderful ginger cat named Wilson (9 years old) is warm, loving company and affection. I'm not sure I would have made it without Wilson."

Enjoying the wide-open spaces of Wyoming with her dog, Julianna of Double Star, WY, said, "My wonderful Golden Retriever, Peanut, is my comfort."

Pets not only bring fun, but a sense of security, especially with children and older adults.

Kelly of Slidell, LA, said, "Our dog has been very good for my aging mother. She absolutely loves my dog! And my dog makes me happy."

As pets age and pass, there is an overwhelming sense of grief fostered by wonderful bonds with the animals. While the pet owners in the survey extolled the joys of owning a pet they also voiced the heartbreak of losing one. These women who have had pets and lost them think twice about getting another one.

Linda of NYC said, "I never wanted a pet because they have a short life span and I would be heart broken when they died. Then I inherited two cats from my brother who couldn't keep them any longer. My husband and I both cried when the dog died. Several years later our daughter asked if we could take care of her dog and we had her for eight years before she died at the age of 14. We were devastated. Cats are entertaining and affectionate when they want something, but dogs are like children each with a distinct personality. They pull on your heartstrings and become a part of your family. They depend on you and you on them. Anyone who asks if you are getting a new dog right after your dog dies, never had a pet."

"It's happiness every day – rain or shine with my Shitzu," said Linda of Indiana.

Elaine of Ashville, AL, shares her home with three horses, two llamas, two dogs, and a cat. "I've always had dogs and often cats. The dogs keep me company, the horses keep me sane. The llamas are just fun to watch. As Winston Churchill said, 'There's something about the outside of a horse that's good for the inside of man.'"

Adding a touch of humor to her response, Lisa of Stratford, CT, noted, " Our dog brings us entertainment, love and SLOBBER!"

Regardless of the breed, pet owners are proud of their dogs and very much aware of the traits and characteristics of the pet they have chosen.

"Our Bassett Hound is sweet, but a lot of work and dog hair," claimed Diane of Randolph, NJ. "Life revolves around him it seems."

Diane of Scituate, RI, no longer has a pet, but she recalls the one she lost. "We did have a Basset Hound, Maggie," she said. "She was a real joy – but sadly she passed away. I could write volumes about this dog – she was funny and loveable."

On the practical side of the pet experience, Mary of Albuquerque, NM, said, "We have two dogs - a Sheppard mix and a lab mix and they encourage us to exercise and be empathetic."

Location – Location – Location

"Jasmine, the name of which signifies fragrance, is the emblem of delicacy and elegance. It is reared with difficulty in New England, but at the south, puts forth all its graces."
~ *Dorothea Dix*

"In Wyoming the beauty of our mountains is matched only by the grit of our people."
~ *Liz Cheney*

"All in all, Vermont is a jewel state, small but precious."
~ *Pearl Buck*

Realtors are famous for explaining the desirability of a home using the mantra: "location, location, location." The same may be said for perspectives when it comes to regional notions.

Many of those who proclaim the south as their birth home will talk about their religion and values differently than their northern counterparts. The same holds true for easterners and westerners.

It would seem that no matter where we live, provincial differences concerning lifestyle, pace of life, weather, history, politics, attitudes toward neighbors, religion, cost of living, and even firearms, vary greatly.

The genteel image of the conservative, cordial southern woman still exists in parts of the south, though not all women are representative of that stereotype.

Tricia of Nashville, TN, balks at the traditional image of southern ladies. "I embrace the southern hospitality, but reject the more conservative social norms, particularly re: women I work with."

Janet, Winston Salem, NC, lives in the south now. "I am replanted from the North. There is more respect and old values here, but that can be good and bad. There is a bit too much Bible belt mentality, but more laidback people friendly. I am friendlier to people because I live with it."

Another southern transplant from the north east, Spring, from Hill, MS, said, "Living here is different – from the speech to the cooking to the seasons. I was raised in the northeast with the bare necessities, so I definitely see a difference living here."

Lyneta of Spring Hill, TN, lived in the south for nine years after living on the west coast. "It was quite a culture shock at first! But here's the things than I enjoy; a friendlier attitude, a slower pace, and less fear of crime. I would say I've become more friendly to people I don't know and more satisfied with a slower pace."

The natural beauty of their environs weighed heavily in responders' descriptions and love of their locale. New Englander Gloria of Wilmington, VT, explained that "living in Vermont is beautiful and very tranquil."

Mary of Albuquerque, NM, said, "The southwest is slower paced with wide open spaces where you always see the horizon, mountains and blue skies."

Besides magnificent, breathtaking scenery, women found their attitudes have been shaped by where they live as well.

Anita from Great Falls, MT, stated that living in the northwest has influenced her way of thinking by making her more "laidback and conservative" than other parts of the country.

Margaret from Derry, NH, is acutely aware of the history of her part of the country. "We are proud New Englanders. My husband's family came over on the Mayflower!"

Where you live may also influence your political agenda.

Jennifer, Scituate, RI, said, "I live in the northeast and am pretty progressive. Spending time with Democrats, artists and intellectuals here has shaped me."

Dartmouth, MA, resident Jasmine was on the same page. "We live in New England and are democratic liberals, hippie environmentalists who are used to enjoying nature outdoors regularly. We are less Yankee direct and aggressive than locals, since we are originally from the Midwest. It's cultural living in a blue state."

Can the weather influence the demeanor and viewpoint of people in a certain state? Maybe, asserts Diane, Dartmouth, MA. "The northeast where I live is very liberal. I think we take pride in the fact that our Revolution started in this part of the country. We can be a bit caustic – but then again we live in a cold, damp climate – that affects everyone's mood."

Though she lives on the opposite coast, Nanette from Surprise, AZ, said, "It's hot here so that certainly affects what we do. There have been times when we went on a short hike to the White Tanks Mountains and considered an annual membership. But, realistically, we would not be able to use it as often as we want due to the heat, rattle snake season, etc. If we lived near the ocean, I think we would be there (even just to stare at it) more often than we step foot outside here."

Barbara of E. Syracuse, NY, explained that the site with its four seasons has had a great influence on her. "Living in a challenging climate makes me feel strong and capable. The distinct seasons give a sense of continuity and dependability."

Barbara lives in Nazareth, PA. "I hate snow and icy winters in the north of Pennsylvania. But I love spring, summer and fall here to do recreational activities."

"Love thy neighbor" is not only a commandment from the Bible. It's a way of life for many of the respondents.

Diane from Anchorage, AK, said, "We are an isolated state and have learned to be self-reliant and independent but to also look out for our neighbors and friends which is a unique aspect in the part of the country where we live."

Caroline from Great Falls, MT, expressed pride in the shared concern for others in her state, where she said stewardship is alive and well. "Living here everyone looks after each other. Families stay close. I think it's because we are not so congested and we are closer to each other."

Lisa from Indianapolis, IN, said, "Living in the midwest for the past 18 years has shown me how much people who need help are there for each other. (Tornado disasters and the poor needing help.)"

Lois of Fairplay, CO, claims that, "Living in the west there are less people, less traffic and people are friendlier. It is a more relaxed atmosphere than many other places."

Phyllis of Fountain Valley, CA, noted that, "I lived in the east, and now I feel much safer here."

A dollar is not worth a dollar in every state. A higher cost of living is what many northeastern women define as a disadvantage of life in this location. Tara, from the Garden State in Hackettstown finds living in the east "harder because there is ever so much more hustle and you have to be more resilient. There is definitely more stress on one's health to live here in addition to higher taxes and car insurances."

Lisa of Stratford, CT, also found the cost of living in the east very high. "It's way too expensive here. I really want to move."

Roxanne of Utah said, "I hate Utah. I am taxed and there are so many things I didn't have to do when I lived in Wyoming. Can't wait to leave the state."

Personal behavior can also be affected by where you call home.

Roberta from Randolph, NJ, said she grew up in the Midwest but has lived in New Jersey many years. "Living in the city's suburbs has made me less wimpy. I can stand up for myself now. Growing up I was more trusting, more polite, and less proactive. I grew up in a black neighborhood that was tough. Had to watch what you said or get beat up. Maybe that's why I wasn't as outspoken. I have southern relatives and lived in the south for seven years and was appalled at the racism still left."

Gail of Magnolia, DE, notes a change in her lifestyle since moving from New Jersey to Delaware. "Growing up on the east coast in the New York/New Jersey metropolitan area, my lifestyle has been ever-moving. I want things done sooner rather than later. Lack of patience. Now, living in what they call 'lower slower Delaware,' I am enjoying the slower pace of life. It's nice to take the time to actually smell the roses."

Tracey of Hackettstown, NJ, says the area in which she lives is conducive to people being serious and uptight. "That's the way the generalized population in the entire northeast is."

Kay, St. Mary's, PA, said, "You don't realize the influence a state has on you until you get out. The people in the east, where I live, are very hard workers and also big eaters. Out west they are more vegan and they are much freer out there."

Not every woman was pleased with her environment.

Eileen of Las Vegas, NV, said, "This area has affected me negatively. My job exposes me to more people who are judgmental and a little racist. I guess I had a sheltered view of the world and now I see the negative side and prejudice."

Religion has been a formative experience for those living in the southern parts of the nation. Why? "It's just there," William Faulkner explained when asked why religion was so vital in his writings.

Elizabeth from Beckley, WV, remarked, "Living in the south definitely influenced my lifestyle. We are in the Bible belt. It's more rural and family oriented."

While the countryside of every state has its inherent beauties and attractions, for some, it means what they feel is a lesser quality in medical care.

Jan from Ridgway, PA, noted that "Living here I feel safer than city life, but there is not enough good medical specialists."

The bright lights of big cities like NYC have attracted many women to its locale.

Linda of NYC, "I grew up and live in New York City. The city has its own peculiar point of view and sense of humor and pride (as do most cities.) Its population has the reputation for being loud, bluntly honest and outspoken. I- think this goes back to the wave of immigrants from different cultures and backgrounds that dared make a new life here against the odds in the early 1900's. This set the cultural values of the city. Many east coast cities are similar. A stereotypical New Yorker is rarely afraid to say exactly what they mean. I have always enjoyed this honesty. It allows a freedom and confidence in having the ability to say, feel and become whatever you want to be. Having lived in Colorado for three years I found the Midwest mentality to be the opposite. The ethnic makeup of the population is more of one background and stricter Christian beliefs. This creates an atmosphere that everyone must think in a similar fashion and hold the same beliefs as everyone else in the community. There was little dialog if a different point of view is expressed. I found this to be stifling. Each section of the country has its own style, and depending on a person's upbringing or comfort range each area can be a wonderful or a horrible experience."

"I expect things done at a hurried pace," explained Linda, another New Yorker, from Flushing. "I expect access to healthcare, transportation, shopping, a variety of services, and assistance with those services on an almost unlimited basis… after all, NY never sleeps. I welcome cultural diversity and willingness to share and experience it. My location affects my lifestyle because it such a place of opportunity and around the clock services and we are known and encourage regarding our outspokenness. I believe it has caused us to expect more… to believe we can achieve more."

Ellen of Mt. Arlington, NJ, said, "Living in the east and close to New York City has made me talk quickly, move quickly and become impatient of those who do not! It has enabled me to take advantage of all New York has to offer."

Marie, another easterner from Flanders, NJ, shared a similar sentiment. "The northeast is an upscale, well educated, high cost area!"

Some women expressed the fact that living in a large city also impacted their outlook on where they lived. "Living in the state's capitol, Indianapolis, I would say we are more business driven," said Pam of Indiana.

A few of the women in the survey maintained that their character has not been influenced by a particular way of life or location.

Rheba of Cincinnati, OH explained, "I live in the Midwest now, but grew up in the southwest. I think maturity has influenced my lifestyle and thinking more than geography."

Anna of Monsey, NY, said the northeast has not changed her lifestyle. "My area doesn't influence me. I'm an individual."

"I was born and raised in Upper Michigan," said Bonnie, Caldwell, ID. "I also spent two years in North Carolina and moved to Idaho to be by family and grandchildren. I've discovered no matter where you live, it's all good."

Biggest Fear

"Nothing in life is to be feared, it is only to be understood. Now is the time to understand more, so that we may fear less."
~ Marie Curie

Women around the world seem to worry about many things. Frequently, these worries transform into genuine fears. The respondents in the survey ranked health, loneliness, and being alone as their primary fears. This was followed by concern for children/grandchildren and spouses.

Several spoke of the fear of losing their job, income, and thus, security.

Anka from Indiana was quite specific in her answer. "I fear getting a terminal illness."

Christy from Edmond, OK, was on the same page in her thinking. "I fear health issues as I grow older, specifically dementia."

Elaine of Ashville, AL, stated, "Getting Alzheimer's or cancer and not being able to see my grandsons grow up. I fear the effects of Obama Ccare and the fact that I am 66 and wonder about Medicare's future."

Having struggled previously with depression, "I fear becoming clinically depressed," said Kathy of Randolph, NJ.

Anita from Great Falls, MT, said, "My biggest fear is living a very confining and pain-filled life due to my allergy to mercury and possibly getting cancer and being denied care under the Obama Ccare Act."

With continuous improvements in medicine, our lives may extend farther than previously indicated. While such a prospect brings hope, it can also elicit anxiety.

"I fear I will live *too long* beyond my capacity to take care of myself," said Barbara of East Syracuse, NY.

Women voiced concern of not only their reaction to a long-term or terminal illness but also the reaction of their loved ones when dealing with such grave issues.

Vicky of Lewes, DE, said, "I hope I do not get a horrible disease and that no one will be willing to assist with my suicide."

Kelly of Slidell, LA, said, "I fear that my son will not be healed from his problem. He's going to jail and my failing to see his problem and get him help has been my failure and source of my fears."

Phyllis of Fountain Valley, CA, said, "I am afraid something terrible will happen to my boys."

"Losing my husband to death even though I know I will join him in heaven one day, is my greatest fear," said Rachel of Downing, MO.

Others, like Martha from Lenexa, KS, said, that in general, "I fear something will happen to me."

The large number of widows and single women aging today presents another side of fears about their solitary situations.

"Being alone in my old age, scares me," said Lisa of Indianapolis, IN "And being alone *and* ill at the same time is frightening."

Many respondents cited mental concerns as much as physical disabilities as an integral part of their trepidation. "I fear health issues as I grow older, specifically dementia," said Christy of Edmonton, OK.

Relationships, marriage, and child rearing as well as the lack of children were other areas of anxiety that were mentioned in the survey.

"I fear not only being alone as I age, but also the fact that I never married," noted Belinda of Portage, IN.

For Cherry of Rosemont, MN, "It's my father I worry about. My mother died in her 50s from lung cancer and she never smoked. Now, I worry about my own kids and what if I die?"

"My greatest fear is losing my husband," said Tricia from Nashville, TN. "Whether from divorce or death, it frightens me."

Elizabeth of Beckley, WV, is also "afraid of losing family members."

For Brie of Clayton, NC, her fears center on her son in the navy. "My biggest fear is that he will have to go to war. I really worry about that."

While some mothers fear for the lives and state of the country, there are others who fear never having children or grandchildren. To them, the future is uncertain without the legacy of children.

Janet from Winston Salem, NC, explained, "I fear not having grandchildren."

Some women feared the loss of their specific animals or confrontation with certain situations. Some of these concerns stem back from childhood or later experiences throughout life.

Janice from Ridgway, PA, stated, "I fear drowning," while Stephanie from Ballantine, MT, fears "Sharks." And for Bonnie of Caldwell, ID, "It's the "dark," while Lenore of Bangor, PA, places her apprehension with "the neighbor next door who owns a lot of guns."

A good number of respondents expressed feelings of uncertainty, fear, and sadness about death. As such, these women cited this as their chief concern in life. Not having time to do what they dreamed of doing, including establishing a career, raising children, and traveling were some of the issues they fretted about to the extreme.

Eileen of Las Vegas, NV, was specific with her answer; "dying young" is the most alarming thing she can imagine.

Being a good parent was paramount to women and thus created a serious unease about their role and effectiveness. "My biggest fear is that I am not a good parent, " noted Lydia of Newark, DE.

"I waited so long to do it that I hate to think I'm screwing it up."

Caryn of Roswell, GA, had similar feelings. "My biggest fear is that I'm not parenting my kids well."

Nannette of Surprise, AZ, was apprehensive about the rising crimes against children in the country. "I fear my children will be kidnapped or a victim of a violent and/or sexual crime."

The loss of a loved one sometimes lessens the fear of death for certain women.

Kathryn of Flanders, NJ, said, "I have lost most of my fears. My great fear was losing my drug-addicted daughter. I've learned fear prevents nothing."

Cindy from Goose Creek, SC, said, "My son passed away before me so I have no more fears."

The state of the economy and employment were a source of anxiety for some, like Diane from Anchorage. "I fear losing my job," she said.

"I fear losing it all," said Jill of Quincy, IL. "I have so much now, friends, family and a job.

For Ana of Monsey, NY, "I am afraid of having no money and being able to survive."

Some women stared fear in the eye. "I don't have any fears," said Pam from Indianapolis, IN.

Thelma of Carry, SC concurred: "I have no fears. I place my trust and destiny exclusively in God."

Gail of Magnolia, DE, believes that "fear is overrated. Usually what you fear does not come to fruition. It takes your joy away. I live in the present and try not to think or fear the future."

Linda from Indianapolis, IN, shared that philosophy. "I have no fears that I can think of that really upset me. I think that living life has given me a sense of 'let the cards fall where they may' and to just keep it moving."

Governmental decisions or the lack of them is what constitutes angst for Barbara of Chester, NJ, "Our government will collapse under Barack Obama. I'm very disappointed in other governing officials for letting the economy get out of hand… mostly disappointed that so many 'important' people are so stupid."

Poor political decisions could very well lead to international conflict.

Diane of Kingstown, RI, said, "I fear another war."

Failure in oneself was mentioned a few times as the core of women's deepest fears.

"It's a tough question; what is my biggest fear," said Linda of NYC. "Fear of failure and disappointing myself for falling short of my goals. I think fear plays a role in being hesitant of trying something new that might be wonderfully life-changing. Moving to Colorado for me was a leap of faith. It didn't work out, but that was okay, so perhaps trying something new is not the problem."

Along a similar line Caroline of South Carolina said, "I'm afraid of starting a family someday and not being able to support it. People are losing their jobs all of the time. That is why I try to save as much as I can and be as frugal as I can."

Disappointments

"You may be disappointed if you fail, but you are doomed if you don't try."

~ Beverly Sills

As trite as it may sound, it's still true: disappointments are a part of our lives. It may come in the form of major losses, such as losing a loved one, not attaining a certain career status, not having children, poor health, and a plethora of other ways in which we feel we have failed not only our family and society, but ourselves as well.

As we age, the crunch to "accomplish" something significant – which varies for each woman – slams into us like a freight train. It's that same old biological clock that ticks the familiar prompt; *hurry up, hurry up.*

Yet what many women fail to understand is that disappointment can be a springboard for better times and can also be a catalyst for achievement. We learn from our mistakes and if what we are seeking – a relationship, a child, a promotion – is sought with deepest passion, then the chances improve for one to acquire what the heart desires.

There is much in life to be disappointed about: the state of the world, poverty, child abuse, crime, political run around, false rhetoric, confusing media stories… and that's just the world view. Within each of us, there are dozens of other issues that can stem from a new career, finding a spouse, healing a wound – physical or psychological – loving oneself, and the drive to forge on no matter the difficulties we face.

The key to disappointment is to keep on trying. Authors, artists, and musicians get numerous rejections before the one *yes*. Teens trying out for a position on a sports team or cheerleading squad must continue their pursuit and not quit. Examine almost any vocation and the possibility of disappointment rears its head.

The respondents cited a wide range of disappointments stemming from the circumstances around them, other people and within themselves.

Taking a humanistic look at her disappointments, Barbara of W. Syracuse, NY, said, "I am disappointed in humanity that people have become violent and hateful to those who are different."

Failed relationships bothered other women.

For Shirley of Manilis, NY, "My greatest disappointment was a failed first marriage."

Money, and the lack of it, contributes to many women's sense of letdown and insecurity.

Anna of Monsey, NY was one such person. "I have no money. The man I love was damaged emotionally and never committed to me in a relationship for more than 30 years. My life is a great disappointment because I'm all alone, have no job and am in poor health."

"Losing my baby was my greatest disappointment," said Rebecca of Missouri. "Also being harassed at work and then fired."

For Nicole in Wisconsin, "Although I've moved on, my greatest disappointment was losing my boyfriend who died in a car crash."

Lynn of Wilmington, DE, stated she worries about her grandchild. "I am disappointed to have a handicapped grandchild who will not live a long life and to have lost two husbands. I fear losing my current companion who is 14 years older than I am."

Brie from Columbia, MD, is a college graduate who works in video sales. "My main disappointment is that I haven't been able to afford to go back to graduate school and have not yet owned a home. I just live paycheck to paycheck at this point."

For Linda of Plainfield, IN, "I am disappointed that I did not have the family and more than one child that I wanted."

"My biggest disappoint is that my husband didn't live to see his grandsons. The fact that I'll probably grow old without a mate is both a fear and a disappointment," said Elaine of Ashville, AL.

Career choice was another source of letdowns.

"I am disappointed that I failed math in college so I couldn't be a science major and an astronaut," said Lydia of Newark, DE.

Lisa of Indiana noted, "I'm disappointed that I didn't follow my own dream from my teen years and listened to others unlike myself. Now I'm on THEIR path not mine."

Disappointment can lead to a poor self-image.

"At times I do not feel like a successful adult," noted Jasmine of Dartmouth, MA. "I do not make a living wage, so cannot live on my own (could not possibly buy my own house, for example). So I live with my mom and am about to move into a house that she has bought. As an unmarried and childless woman in my mid-thirties I judge myself as not having accomplished the goals most people have. I want to be married, and someday adopt a child."

Anka of Avon, IN, agreed. "I'm disappointed that I didn't have more education and also a failed marriage."

Knowing one can't go back in time and squeeze every bit of experience with a loved one who has passed, affects many of us.

"I am disappointed that I didn't spend more time with my mother while she was living," said Caryn of Roswell, GA.

Timing was a source of disappointment for Nannette of Surprise, AZ. "I'm disappointed that I didn't have my kids earlier and I put up with so much crap from their father before then."

Many women rue their earlier years when their priorities were different.

Jennifer of Scituate, RI, said, "I am disappointed that I spent so much of my energy focused on boyfriends in my twenties."

Personal relationships played a key role in contributing to Jeanie of Honolulu, HI's sense of frustration and disappointment. "Two things: one was my husbands' family treated me badly from the moment of his funeral in every way in general after it. They were vicious with no decency. Another disappointment was another man before I was going to marry him had sex with other people."

Bonnie of Caldwell, ID, explained her disappointment, which "lies in my trying too much to please other people."

Christy from Edmonton, OK, said, "I am disappointed that I paid too much attention to things that don't really matter or make a difference."

Some of the women had societal disappointments.

"I am disappointed that so many mothers can't devote more time to raising and mothering their children," noted Norma of Chester, NJ.

Children were a source of disappointment for some.

Roberta of Randolph, NJ, said, "I'm disappointed that my child does not have the same ethical morality as us."

In a similar vein, Janet of Winston-Salem, NC, said, "I'm disappointed when my kids don't work and live to their potential and settle for less than they should."

Pat of Arvada, CO, said she is "disappointed I chose the wrong father for my children."

"My son dying and not being in our lives," said Peggy of Dover, NJ.

Rheba of Cincinnati, OH, said, "I'm disappointed and wish that I could have given my children more social advantages when they were growing up. I could have had a membership in a community pool, but felt we couldn't afford it. I should have found the money for that."

Health also was an issue.

Frances of Fargo, ND said, "I'm disappointed at having arthritis and asthma."

Heather of Verona, WI, stated she was disappointed in her marriage, while Liz of Goose Creek, SC, said, "That I never had a daughter."

Sheila of Tannersville, PA, said "That I didn't make up a bucket list earlier in life."

Ana of Monsey NY, concludes, "My whole life is a great disappointment since I'm all alone and poor."

Dreaming Big

"When you have a dream you've got to grab it and never let go."

~ Carol Burnett

There is such a thing as dreaming safe and dreaming big. Women who participated in the survey conveyed both types of dreaming. These imaginings range from the usual hopes for career advancement, happiness, travel, and improved health to more humanitarian and exotic notions.

Rachel of Peak's Island, ME's fondest dream is to travel with her son globally and have an extended period of non-working time with him. "It will be a while due to finances till this can become a reality."

Cherry from Minnesota seeks a relationship. "My fondest dream is to find a father figure, an ideal dad for my kids, but I have no idea when that will happen."

Spring of Walls, MS, hopes to "someday own my own business revolving around my sewing."

Rachel of Downing, MO's fondest dream "is to have a baby which God will decide."

The artistic side of her nature is what motivates graphic artist Nicole of Pittsburgh, PA. "My dream is to create something, a comic, cartoon or game that people love."

Linda of NYC responded with, "That's a good question. I always say my life is full of five-year plans that change every year. At present I would like to get away from computers and back into more tactile art. Creating handmade crafts to sell on Etsy to various shops and travel to different craft fairs around the country. Ideally, sell everything and travel the country in a van."

Gail of Magnolia, DE's fondest dream is "to write a story to help people find their connection with God. Not sure that will ever be, but it's my dream."

Lynetta of Spring Hill, TN, has a similar goal. "I dream of moving beyond publishing articles and stories to have a book contract."

Tricia of Nashville, TN, said, "I dream of achieving professional success and advance biomedical research at a level that is recognized nationally and that my family is very proud of me."

Linda of Plainfield, IN, said, "My fondest dream is to have a book published. And hopefully it will happen within two years."

Martha of Lenexa, KS, says "I dream of getting my certification and working in a hospital."

Mila of New Jersey also geared her response to her deeply religious belief. "My fondest dream is to bypass Purgatory."

For Caroline of South Carolina, "I want to have a fairytale wedding, and build a cabin and raise a family there."

Location is a priority for some women.

Liz of Goose Creek, SC, says, "I want to live and die on a beach."

Tracey of Hackettstown, NJ, was more nostalgic in her choice. "Someone cradling my face in their hands telling me they love me and kissing me like it could be our last kiss, that is my dream."

Some wished to be in heaven with passed loved ones.

"Going to heaven and being reunited with my own family and other loved ones," said Shirley of Manilas, NY.

Mary of Albuquerque, NM, said, "Seeing my mother driving a school bus opening the door, telling me everything was going to be alright and 'hop on in.' I feel my mother is watching over me along with the rest of our family every day."

Financial improvement was also cited as a fervent dream for some.

"I dream of not having to live paycheck to paycheck," commented Brie of Columbia, MD.

For 93-year-old Dorothy of Kenilworth, NJ, it's "becoming a millionaire and living forever."

Lorraine of Hackettstown, NJ, was altruistic in her answer, saying, "A world where there is no war, no hunger and no suffering where we live in peace and good health and no one is judged for the color of their skin."

Some women, like Elaine of Ashville, AL, were all about learning a skill that could benefit others. She said, her dream consists of "mastering Spanish and becoming an interpreter for mission trips to and movies set in Latin American countries, and maybe one starring or directed by George Clooney?? Hopefully my dream will be fulfilled in a year or two since I'm planning on studying Spanish for a month in Costa Rica. I already speak the language, but have been stuck at the intermediate level for years. I'm hoping the month in CR will help me become fluent."

A few women indicated they are living their dream through their jobs.

For Pat of Sandyston, NJ, "I dream of still working. I'm 87 and still at it."

"I love that I am dedicated to a career that aligns with my passions," said Jasmine of Dartmouth, MA. "I aspire to someday do more marine biology and climate change education."

Parents' Impact on You

"My parents must have done a great job. Anytime I wanted to pursue something that they weren't familiar with, that was not part of their lifestyle, they let me go ahead and do it."
~ *Sally Ride, first female astronaut in space*

"The relationship between parents and children, but especially between mothers and daughters, is tremendously powerful, scarcely to be comprehended, in any rational way."
~ *Joyce Carol Oates*

Most people would agree that parenting goes far beyond meeting the basic necessities for offspring. While it is doubtless vital to feed, clothe, and educate our children, it is also assumed that parents will love, instruct, and guide their children into a satisfying adulthood. The influence exerted on how their children turn out, including their personality, work ethic, emotional development, and behavior is a foregone conclusion. And this is true whether that child rearing experience was wonderful or abysmal.

All of the respondents agreed their parents impacted their lives; some for the better, some for the worse. And both parents had their share of input on their growth.

"My dad was always practical yet made time for fun," said Mary of Albuquerque NM. "My mother was extremely social and taught me to be generous and outgoing with people."

Rachel, from Downing, MO, said, "In more ways than I can list my parents have influenced my lifestyle choices. They are my role models!"

Caryn of Roswell, GA, credited her parents with having a positive influence on her lifestyle. "My mom taught me so much; to have drive, fight for what you believe, stand up for yourself and be proud of who you are. My dad – patience, always do your best and he is still working on teaching me to love history, but that just hasn't quite happened …"

The degree of discipline and outlook took a toll on some of the respondents. Some perceived their upbringing made them too sheltered or too harsh in terms of advice and direction. In either case, the women claimed they had learned from those mistakes.

For Rachel, Peaks Island, ME, "My parents have always been unlimited in the love, and support with a dose of practicality, sometimes too much precautionary based in fear. I wish I had learned better to act less out of fear."

A dose of skepticism was part of Jeanine of Honolulu, HI's parental advice. "My mother taught me to be responsible and didn't trust people because they would cheat me. As a result, I tended to be more judgmental and critical. -

Hackettstown, NJ, resident, Tracey noted that, "My parents were not risk takers and I tend to be cautious and do things the safest way I can."

In some instances, the women indicated that budgetary issues influenced the direction they were forced to pursue upon completing a high school education.

Kay of St. Mary's, PA, wanted to go to college. "My parents insisted soon as I got out of high school I had to get a job and support myself. I pleaded with them, please, please let me go to college. The first part of my senior year I took a test for a scholarship to get financial help. I didn't know where to go and dad got extremely mad. 'Don't think you have home to come back to,' he said. I was an insecure teenager and didn't know what to do. It put dampers on everything. Then again I prayed every night to get a job and one day my dad comes home and says his company has an opening. He told me my first paycheck had to go to the church. It was a hard experience for me."

Though money was an issue at Roxanne's home, it didn't changed the closeness of the family or drive out anyone's ambitions. "The love and us being close even if we didn't have money was key," the Utah resident said. "Even if we didn't have money we had lots of love and fun times camping and being together."

Morality played a role in the family life of certain women.

Pam of Indianapolis, IN, said, "I would say religion and respect for my elders were taught to me by my parents. They taught us to follow the Golden Rule and I would say they instilled good values."

Telia of Bowling Green, KY, recalls "They helped me plant roots in southern Kentucky. They helped me understand the value of a dollar, the importance of family, and the truth that we sometimes need to find solace in our own bubble to create the reality we'd want to live."

"My parents were fair and open minded and led by example," said Janet, Winston-Salem, NC. "They did the right thing and taught us to do the same. They had respect for themselves and lived with dignity without judging, I try to do the same."

Certain parents emphasized the importance of a good education.

"They were hard working and emphasized the importance of getting a college education and were widely traveled," said Diane of Anchorage, AK.

Several women admitted they towed the line as their parents wished.

Caroline of Great Falls, MT, said, "My parents wanted education for us kids and we did that. They wanted us to stay close and we did that. They wanted us to help each other and others and we did that too."

Linda of Indianapolis, IN, said, "My mother influenced my lifestyle by teaching me to be strong, kind (until you have to be unkind) think for yourself and NOT be a follower. This influence came from a mother who only had a sixth grade education – maybe not a lot of BOOK sense, but a whole lot of COMMON sense."

Sometimes parents who are not "with the times" can be frustrating to their children.

Belinda from Portage, IN explained, "My parents were very old fashioned. They are stuck back behind their picket fence and don't know what it is to 'go online' or any technology."

Jasmine of Rhode Island said, "My parents influenced me in many ways! They encouraged me to explore nature and think like a scientist as a child and nurtured a love of coastal biology. They raised me mostly vegetarian and encouraged critical thinking, all leading to my political leanings and environmentalism."

Not all responses recalled positive memories.

Alyssia of San Pedro, CA, noted, "My parents lives' impacted on me, for sure. My dad was on drugs and my mom was an alcoholic. We went through a lot of hardships until I was 26."

Linda from Plainfield, IN, said, "I feel like you can only count on yourself and that has made me very independent."

Saralynn of Dakota City, NE, said her parents influence was a good lesson for her. "My parents showed me what NOT to do."

Barbara of Irvington, NJ, said her parents were German immigrants. Her mother ran a day care service in their home. "When I found out I was pregnant at 16, I hid it. She didn't know until I started going into labor at home. She would not let me put him up for adoption because she wanted to punish me for not being married or finishing high school. But the worst was that for his whole life she kept telling my son, her grandson, that he was a mistake. This affected him and at one point while playing with matches he set part of the house on fire. In later years, he went to jail. I should have adopted him out. We all would have had a better life."

Gloria of Vermont was insistent, "I don't want to be like my mom."

Learning from her parents mistakes, Nashville, TN, resident Tricia, commented, "In my family I now model my focus on family time, involvement with my children. I also work harder at communications than my parents. I am more open/forthcoming with my children."

There were some women who were adamant about not repeating their mother and father's parenting. "I did not want to mirror my parents' relationship and I haven't," said Tania of Annapolis, MD.

Lynetta of Spring Hill, TN, said, "I've embraced the good parts – strong work ethic, etc. but basically gone the opposite direction of their values."

Lisa of Flushing, NY, said, "My mom and grandma drummed into my head that I should never depend on anyone so I rely on myself. They taught me that I could do anything I put my mind to so I persevere (most of the time!) They taught me to speak up, so I'm assertive… and… brutally honest, at all times, with the appropriate respect required, depending on whom I'm brutalizing with the truth at the time! … Grandma didn't understand the significance of a true friend and treating them as family because she grew up in a big family and family was IT… from that I learned what family should mean and what a true friend really means… friends are choices, family isn't. If I call you a good friend, it means you are like family. I value my relationships with my friends immensely. From watching the dysfunctional relationships of my parents, and the very functional relationship of my grandparents, I learned what type of relationships I wanted and which to be careful not to fall prey to and how to maintain a healthy relationship. Fortunately, I made the right choices and my husband and friends all share the same mindset about the importance of good relationships."

Cindy of Goose Creek, SC, commented, "My parents always told me if you want something, work for it. And don't give up."

Heather of Verona, WI, noted, "My parents have influenced my lifestyle choices in every way. They have still a happily married beautiful home and raised me and my sister to be respectable people and follow in the footsteps by getting a career, supporting myself and doing everything correct."

"Always being there for me," is what Elizabeth of Beckley, WV, remembers about her parents' influence on her lifestyle.

"My parents instilled in me my work ethic as well as the need to first be honest with myself," said Neva of Des Moines, WA. "My word is my bond."

Sports

"People want to think that staying in shape costs a lot of money. They couldn't me more wrong. It doesn't cost anything to walk. And it's probably a lot cheaper to go to the corner store and buy vegetables than take a family out for fast food."

~ Florence Griffith Joyner

These days, women are less likely to be saddled with the nomenclature of "football/baseball widow." Rather than be abandoned by partners who are glued to the baseball diamond at a ball field or the television screen, they are either right alongside them or are participating in a sport on their own.

Females account for more than a third of 14 million-plus people that tune into major sporting events, like the NBA finals, World Series, Daytona 500, and Stanley Cup Finals according to data from Nielson. And as for the granddaddy sporting event of the year, the Super Bowl, the 2011 figures jumped to 45.0 percent of the 111 million viewers, or some 50 million, being women cheering on the two teams.

"I don't think people realize how big a percentage of fans are women," said Stephen Master, a Nielsen vice president. And this is nothing new. He notes that women have been a big part of the viewing audience for the better part of the last decade for major events.

How did our women rank? Those women, who indicated some interest in sports, either observing a sport or participating, totaled 41 percent, in comparison to 68.9 percent who declared no interest in sports whatsoever. Some were fans of a single sport, others only their children's recreational sports or college athletics.

Many of the women who responded to the survey enjoy rooting for their favorite major league football team right alongside their partners. One such person is Alyssia of San Pedro, CA, who loves the Dodgers and Raiders. Her basketball pick? "That's easy," she said. "The Lakers without a doubt."

Christy of Edmond, OK, is pro Syracuse Orange basketball, the NY Yankees and the Buffalo Bills, while Lisa of Stamford, CT, is a fan of the San Francisco 49ers and the Jets and roots for the Mets as her favorite baseball team.

Others put themselves literally behind the wheel when it comes to participating in sports. When time permits, Bonnie, Caldwell, ID enjoys NASCAR driving with her husband. "On television we also watch hockey, football and baseball as well," she said.

Quite a few women noted they regularly bike, horseback ride, and hike, with some being swim and/or dance/aerobics instructors at local YMCAs. All were avid fans of their children/grandchildren's sports participation. Many of these women faithfully follow the Olympic Games as well.

Living in one part of the country does not prohibit women from cheering on teams from other regions of the nation. From way down south in Clermont, FL, Linda is a huge fan of the New England Patriots, while Thelma of Cary, NC, claims "The Miami Heat are THE best basketball team!"

"The Seattle Sea Hawks is my football team," said Krystal of Dickinson, ND.

True to her homeland, Jasmine of Dartmouth, MA, supports the Red Sox baseball and New England Patriots in football. "I also am a fan of gymnastics and volleyball during the Olympics."

Other women were more focused fans of college or local teams. Those women cited political tactics as one reason for vanquishing professional athletes from their interests. Instead, they look to collegiate athletics for the thrill and excitement of rooting for a team.

Diane of Anchorage AK, roots for her favorite college football and basketball teams, the California Golden Bears. She also watches tennis and most Olympic sports.

Tricia of Nashville, TN, enjoys, "mostly my college (Vanderbilt) basketball, baseball and football."

Caryn of Roswell, GA, is a big fan of Auburn, while Janet, Winston-Salem, NC, supports the University of NC basketball, University of SC football and Army football.

Finally, there is no fan like a parent or grandparent when it comes to watching children and grandchildren display their athletics.

Norma of Chester, NJ said, "While I enjoy college football and basketball more than the pros, I also really enjoy seeing my grandchildren participate in their sports."

Culture

> *"The arts are not a frill. The arts are a response to our individuality and our nature, and help to shape our identity. What is there that can transcend deep difference and stubborn divisions? The arts. They have a wonderful universality. Art has the potential to unify. It can speak in many languages without a translator. The arts do not discriminate. The arts can lift us up."*
> ~ *Former Texas Congresswoman Barbara Jordan*

During the Victorian age only the well-to-do had the means and opportunity to indulge in the arts. A lot has changed in that area. Women have taken center stage in their support of cultural events across the country. The majority of the women in the survey indicated their interest in the arts, though some sadly admitted their financial situation could and has prevented them from participating as much as they would like. High ticket prices were cited as the chief reason they and their families refrain from frequent attendance.

All agree that living in or near a city that values recreation, art, and cultural events is important to the entire family. *Property Shark*, a property research website, put together a list of the top 20 US cities that offer the most cultural activities. This includes museums, libraries, theaters, parks and stadiums. The top 10 include Seattle, WA; Indianapolis, IN; Miami area, FL; Houston, TX; Boston, MA; Columbus, OH; San Antonio, TX; Philadelphia, PA; Charlotte, NC; and Washington, D.C. New York City ranked 13 on the top 20 list.

Just how popular are the arts? In the 2014-2015 seasons, there were a record breaking 13.1 million admissions to Broadway shows with 68 percent of the audience female. The average Broadway theatergoer reported attending four shows in the previous 12 months. And in keeping with statistics, it seems that interest is intergenerational. Ticketmaster's 2014 live event attendance study found that Baby Boomers 55 and over accounted for just 22 percent of concert goers while the 18 to 34 group accounted for 35 percent, and middle-aged groups 35 to 54 were 43 percent of attendees. The most active concert goers were those in the 35-54 -year old age range.

While there is little doubt that the arts are popular, they are for many, no longer affordable. This is evidenced by box office sales. New studies released by the National Endowment for the Arts and based on surveys carried out in 2012 claim that arts attendance in the US has continued to drop over the past two decades, but both struggle to incorporate digital activities into their findings. These studies, "A Decade of Arts Engagement: Findings from the survey of public participation in the Arts 2002 – 2012" and "When Going Gets Tough: Barriers and Motivations Affecting Arts Attendance," break down arts attendance, participation, and production figures demographically and attempt to account for the reasons certain groups do and don't attend cultural events.

For example, the number of visitors to the "core" arts, opera, jazz, classical music, ballet, musical theater, plays, art museums and galleries, continue to decline with 33.4 percent of US adults attending one of these between 2011 and 2012. A decade earlier, it was 39.4 percent.

The women in our survey reflected this ebb in cultural actives. Most cited affordability and time as issues which resulted in their nonattendance. According to the responses, 33.3 percent of the women said they attend some form of cultural event (museum, theater, concert, movie) less than three times a year, while 9.2 percent attend three events per year. Additionally, 33.9 percent claim they attend more than three events per year as compared to 32.7 percent who said they never participate in these social activities.

At issue in part is the government cutbacks to the arts, which can lead to rising ticket prices. The higher rates make, for those on a tight budget, the arts – museums, theater, musical concerts, and movies – prohibitive or very limited.

Things have not improved in this area. Over the past couple of decades, the National Endowment for the Arts has been dutifully tracking the gradual decline in attendance at cultural events. As part of a series of reports released in January 2015, the federal agency decided to augment its latest update by focusing on two key questions: How many people seriously have considered attending a play, concert, or art exhibit, only to finally pass? And why did they end up staying home?

The answers to these questions are surprising. While cost certainly made the list, it was less of a factor than a lack of time. And for some, the inaccessibility – the perception that the venue where an event is held would be too difficult to get to – was cited nearly as often as money. In addition, one in five decided to stay home because "they could not find anyone to accompany them."

In the majority of cases the women respondents were most likely inclined to focus of financial aspects of attendance to events as opposed to going alone or living too far away.

Linda has homes in both New York City and Colorado. "I'm able to manage classical concepts about twice a year. Museums several times a year; theater or opera, rarely. Enjoy Cirque de Soleil about every three years. Movies, never. There is no movie made today that is worth the $10 to $15 price."

Caroline of Great Falls, MT, has her movie and saves money too. "We watch movies on TV. I actually don't enjoy going out at night."

Health issues sometimes deter appreciating the arts as well. Rheba of Cincinnati, OH, said, "We used to do concerts, theater, movies and museums frequently, but now with my husband's vision and hearing issues which are greatly impaired, we seldom go out and I rarely go alone."

Of all of the arts mentioned, women were most likely to take in movies one to three times a year citing high cost of theater tickets and concerts as reasons not to attend.

Ellen of Mt. Arlington, NJ, loves the theater. "We subscribe to a local theater which features concerts, plays, etc. and take advantage of the proximity to New York theater whenever we can."

Yet some women go to the movies often.

Linda of Clermont, FL said she attends movies once a month and theater one a year. Peggy of Dover, NJ, said she goes to the movies every week, and Margaret of Derry, NH, goes quite often. Saralynn of Dakota City, NE, sees a movie twice a month.

For Jeanine of Honolulu, HI, "It's movies once a week for me. I never go to museums and concerts and theater rarely, but I love my movies."

Nanette of Surprise, AZ, waits each year for two concerts. "Rock and Worship Road Show and Winger Jam made up of 10 different Christian artists/bands. It cost $10 and though price is not the motivating factor in our attendance, I usually get a suite for my kids youth group. I love to stand there and look out over what is my home away from home and watch people worshipping together. It is indescribable."

Lydia of Newark, DE, is all about art and museums. "I try to go at least three times a year."

She is not alone. Lisa of Indianapolis, IN, visits museums three or more times a year as well.

"We do concerts, movies, theater and art numerous times a year," said Tania of Annapolis, MD. "Definitely more than three times annually."

Lorraine of Hackettstown, NJ, has "never been to a theater, movies maybe once a year and never had a vacation."

Anna of Monsey, NY stated, "I have no money and can't go to anything. But I do watch concerts and plays on television. I make do with what I can."

America: One Language for All?

"We can send a message and say, 'you want to be in America, A, you'd better be here legally or you're out of here. B, when you're here, let's speak American. Let's speak English, and that's a kind of a unifying aspect of a nation is the language that is understood by all."

~ Former Alaska Governor and Republication VP nominee, Sarah Palin

A Rasmussen poll released in 2014 indicated that 83 percent of those participating say that English should be the official language of the United States. The interesting thing is that the country, to date, has no official language on the books.

Making English the official language is a hot bed issue. While doing so would encourage new migrants to learn the language of the country they have accepted as their own, others contest the large influx should dictate a duality of languages. The **English-only movement**, also known as the **Official English movement**, maintains that only the English language is the language of the United States.

Ironically, while many people think English IS the official language, it isn't so. The United States has never had a legal policy proclaiming an official national language. However, at some times and places, there have been various moves to promote or require the use of English. As one of the major centers of commerce and trade, and a major English-speaking country, many assume that English is the country's official language. But despite efforts over the years, the United States has no official language.

The women in the survey had very specific reasons for their choice as to whether to make Spanish a second official language of the nation. Opposing the notion were 74 percent of the respondents. Advocates for such a notion totaled 10.7 percent, while 15.1 percent were completely "unsure."

According to the American Civil Liberties Union (ACLU), English-only laws are inconsistent with both the First Amendment right to communicate with or petition the government, as well as free speech and the right to equality because they bar government employees from providing non-English language assistance and services.

On August 11, 2000, President Bill Clinton signed Executive Order 1316, "Improving Access to Services for Persons with Limited English Proficiency." The executive order requires federal agencies to examine the services they provide, identify any need for services to those with limited English proficiency (LEP) and develop and implement a system to provide those services so LEP persons can have meaningful access to them.

While the judicial system has noted that state English-only laws are largely symbolic and non-prohibitive, others in managerial positions often interpret them to mean English is the mandatory language of daily life. Of course, there are pros and cons to creating bi-lingual nations. But there are also benefits of making English the sole language. Some assert it would save billions in federal spending. The cost of translators and bilingual education alone are billions and many are born by local governments.

In LA in 2002, for example, $15 million or 15 percent of the election budget was devoted to printing ballots in seven languages and hiring bilingual poll workers. In 2000, Executive Order 13166, which forces health care providers who accept Medicare and Medicaid payments to hire interpreters for any patient who requires one, at the providers' own cost.

Many second-generation immigrants who don't speak English find themselves negatively affected in the job market. Learning English opens doors to move up the socioeconomic ladder. While the media often speaks of the need for everyone to speak another language, often Spanish, the women here take pride in their nation's language: English. Many felt that if someone chooses to live here, they should be the ones who must assimilate to the language of America.

Of the women who participated in the survey 74.3 percent said English should be the official language of the United States; 15.3 percent were "unsure" and 10.8 percent said that the nation should be bi-lingual with Spanish as the designated second official language.

The women had sensible explanations for their beliefs.

Elaine of Ashville, AL, said "Despite my love of Hispanics and their language, I believe one official language should be English. It's very expensive to print instructions, etc. in another language. It's easier to assimilate when everyone speaks the same and it's a matter of tradition. We started as an English-speaking country."

Diane from Anchorage, AK, explained, "English is our mainstay. Language is what unifies a country and culture, although I think everyone should be multilingual."

Lynn from Wilmington, DE, was on the same page. "No, we should not make Spanish one of our official languages. It is divisive. Other languages should be encouraged but everyone should understand English."

Lydia, from Newark, DE, agrees. "When I visited a family in Germany I did my best to learn to speak that language. I didn't expect them to speak English. I think people who come to America should speak English. However, I also believe that America should have the interest in speaking other languages."

Linda from Clermont, FL, said, "If I went to France I would need to speak French not expect them to speak English."

Caryn from Georgia was even more adamant about maintaining a one language country by mandating official classes for immigrants. "Absolutely not; I firmly believe that one should speak English to live in the US and show proof they are in classes learning it."

Roxanne of Utah said, "We should only have American spoken because this is the USA and English is and should be the only language spoken here."

While Rachel of Peaks Island, ME, concedes that "we should educate our children to be bi-lingual at a younger age," she does not view mandatory dual languages.

Heather of Verona, WI, interjected another salient point. "I don't think being bilingual here would be easy. All federal employees would also have to learn the other language and printing of materials would cost a lot in the budget."

Lorraine of Hackettstown, NJ, commented, "I think what makes each country unique are the things that they were founded on including the original language not to mention because this is a melting pot to be fair would have to adopt EVERY language of every culture living here."

Great Falls, MT, resident Anita said, "This is America NOT USA Mexico or USA Muslim. English is our language and if you come here to live then learn our language and customs. If you don't want to learn English then stay in your own country!"

If the policies for immigration were good enough when our ancestors came to America, they should be good enough for immigrants now, was the sentiment expressed by Jeanine of Honolulu, HI. "It's ridiculous to determine a second language like Spanish should be official because my great grandma's German and had to learn English. We can't change practices for invading illegal immigrants."

History is on the side of those who favor an English-only policy. Several of the women noted the Pilgrims were English and brought the language with them to the new world, thus making it our founding language.

Christy from Edmond, OK said, "English was the original language – I see no need to force a second language. But I do think learning a language should be part of high school education for all."

Sue of Lake Hopatcong, NJ, said, "I don't speak Spanish. I speak English. Why should we have Spanish as a second language?"

Gloria from Wilmington, VT, explained, "My family background is Hungarian and I did not speak English when I started school. But I learned."

Mila of Chester, NJ, also recalled coming to the USA from the Philippines, and "I learned English. There was no one to say, let's make Philippine the language."

Cherry of Rosemont, MN, had similar thoughts. "I was born in the Philippines and I learned to speak English before I came here. How could the country choose one language over another? Spanish vs. Philippine??"

Some women were on the fence about the language issue.

Lisa of Indianapolis, IN, admitted, "I am not sure yet. I do believe it melds our differences and is an attribute to know two languages. In the US it probably would be Spanish because of the influx of Latinos. I don't think, however, that the US is as a whole ready for it."

"I have mixed feelings about this," said Gail of Magnolia, DE. "I'm all for people learning more than one language like many of the European countries. But I do believe English should be first and foremost. English is this country's original roots."

In the minority of the survey, were the 10 percent of women who were all for making Spanish the official second language of the United States.

Margie of Randolph, NJ said, "Sure; the more we can communicate with more people the better. The other language could perhaps be the one that most people speak to start with."

Kathy of Randolph, NJ, said, sardonically "Sure, we should have another language as an official one. How about Cherokee? After all, they were here first."

Some of the women were very enthusiastic about having Spanish declared a second language of the country. Indianapolis, IN, resident Linda said, "I definitely think the USA should become a bi-lingual country and I think Spanish is the way to go. This is the way of the world which is very diverse with people of all ethnicities in the USA who continue to come here and I don't see this trend changing in the future in any way."

Vicky of Lewes, DE, responded with, "Why not? We've always been a melting pot."

Linda from NYC thought it was a fine idea to have Spanish as a second official language of record for the USA and took an historical view of the issue. "The Spanish and the French colonies were as much a part of the development of this country as were the English. To ignore that is to ignore the history of the country… Having a one-language country also feeds into a continued ignorance of its present population."

"I would not object to the USA being a bi-lingual country officially," said Jasmine of Dartmouth, MA. "I would guess it would be Spanish."

Jean of Sciota, PA, asks, "Why not Spanish?"

Kay of St. Mary's, PA, thought, "It's good for everyone to know a second language. Everyone in Europe is fluent in more than one language, especially English."

Jennifer of Scituate, RI, agreed that the US should become a bilingual country. "Spanish would be nice. We should all be able to communicate with our neighbors."

For some women, the notion of Spanish as a second language is already a moot point.

Pamela of Flanders, NJ, notes that "I think we are all heading in that direction where Spanish will become a second language here. It is so important to be accepting of people. Learning a new language is good for the brain and can be an asset to all."

Retirement

"Retirement is not in my vocabulary. They aren't ever going to get rid of me that way."
                                                     ~ Betty White

The concept of retirement can be a welcome or frightening one. Depending on financial status, love of a job, health issues, babysitting grandchildren, community involvement, and a sense of wanderlust, it can mean – to borrow the Dickensian phrase – either the best of times or the worst of times.

For many, money is the bottom line and key to their successful yet enjoyable retirement.

"My husband just retired and I believe we will be just fine. We might have to cut back on our traveling, though," said Mary of Albuquerque, NM.

Kay of St. Mary's, PA, said, "We are already retired and we watch our money. We both get allowances and do what we want with it. I kept a horse and two hunting dogs. Now I have started a business and go on trips and he uses his funds for hunting and fishing."

Judy from Indian Lakes, SC, says she is also organized and credits her southern residence as an asset. "We are retired and fairly-well prepared. We also live in the South which is so much less expensive."

Tricia from Nashville, TN, says she is more prepared than most people. "But I worry it still might not be good enough to support travel which we would enjoy."

Neva of Des Moines, WA, says she and her husband have been prepared for the last 18 years. "So far, we are doing alright."

Gloria from Wilmington, VT, said "We just roll with the punches when it comes to our retirement." She did indicate they have prepaid their final expenses and have a will in place.

Hannah of Killington, VT, said the proceeds from her sale of her inn should, when the time comes, ease any future financial stress during retirement.

Becca of West Plains, MO, said, "I'm working really hard to get the house paid off. I have no other major debt. I figure I will work till I'm 70 so I can receive $400 more a month from Social Security benefits."

Some of the women noted while they are prepared for retirement, their husbands and partners are not.

New Yorker Shirley said, "I am retired and am doing well. He is not."

Eileen of Las Vegas, NV, explained, "I guess we're okay."

Utah resident Roxanne said, "We've taken care of our burial plan and are prepared for retirement."

Lynetta of Spring Hill, TN notes, "We've got a good plan for retirement and have made all the arrangements for final expenses and written down instructions."

Tricia of Nashville, TN, said, "We've prepare better than most, but I still worry it might not be good enough to support travel we would enjoy."

Jennifer of Scituate, RI said, "We're on the right track. We're also working on final expense plans."

Barbara of Nazareth, PA, explained, "We've finished our plans for retirement. Just deciding when to finish working and play. Have made wills and designated plots for burial after cremation."

"My husband is not as mentally prepared for retirement. I was well prepared both mentally and financially," said Rheba of Cincinnati, OH. "We've also done the will and the guardians and I have made final resting plans."

Being prepared usually implies women have reached a certain age. Those over 50 have had time to think about retirement since at least some of their family's expenses – tuition, mortgages – have been lowered or paid off. It also means that many are empty nesters, no longer needing to support children.

And then there were the younger women just starting careers and families.

Amanda of Rapid City, ND, is not at all prepared for retirement. "I am only in my 20s," she explained.

Garden State resident Amanda, also in her 20s, has no retirement plans in place nor does Courtney from Queens City, MO.

Stacey from Garwood, NJ, who has two teenagers at home said, "We are actively planning and at this time a life insurance policy is all that has been decided on."

Final Decisions

"I don't want to have lived in vain like most people. I want to be useful or bring joy to all people, even those I've never met. I want to go on living, even after my death!"

~ Anne Frank

The younger the women, the less chance they have cemented retirement plans or made decisions for their final resting place. Sensing they have more time to plan, and compounded with present financial situations like schooling, children, education costs, insurance, house mortgages, and car loans, they feel able to shelve such decisions.

An example of this thinking was raised by Rachel from Peaks Island, ME, who is raising a young child by herself. "At this point retirement and final preparations are a luxury and not one I can afford."

Kathy from Randolph, NJ, said, "Not prepared at all for retirement or final resting place plans. I'll be working till death knocks at my door!"

North Carolinian Caroline said she and her partner have a 401-k plan and "plan to add to it until we retire. As far as final resting sites, we are both still very young (20s) and haven't really thought about it yet."

Sarah from Chester, NJ, said, "We are trying hard to prepare but feel like we can never retire. As to final expenses, we are just starting to discuss and this is SO scary!"

Rheba of Cincinnati, OH, claims, "I was well prepared and ready, both mentally and financially, however my husband not as mentally. He still fights it."

Gun Control

"There is a lot of talk now about metal detectors and gun control. Both are good things. But they are no more a solution than forks and spoons are to world hunger."
                                                        ~ Anna Quindlen

In a story in the NJ Star Ledger, "Divided We Stand," April 28, 2014, it was reported that some 60 percent of households in Montana own guns compared to 13 percent in Rhode Island. To maintain that the issue of gun control is a divided one is an obvious understatement.

Over the past few years, multiple schools across the US have been impacted by shootings, which have resulted in the deaths of both students and faculty members. Those who staunchly favor limiting the number of weapons quickly point to the site of such school shootings in Florida, Connecticut, Kentucky, California, New Mexico, and the list goes on.

But tragically, the gun violence isn't limited to schools. Movie theaters like the one in Aurora, CO, and concerts like the one at Mandalay Bay, Las Vegas, have been the targets for gun-related massacres. In a report by Jen Christensen for CNN, Oct. 5, 2017, a study by Adam Lankford, professor of criminal justice at the University of Alabama, claims that while the United States has 5 percent of the world's population, it had 31 percent of all public mass shootings.

Concealed carry and open carry of guns varies by state. Some states allow residents to carry handguns without permits. But 44 of our states have a provision in their state constitutions similar to the nation's Second Amendment which protects the right to keep and bear arms.

Roberta from Randolph, NJ sees both sides of the issue. "I'm half southern (Texas) so have used guns in the past, mainly killing coyote who preyed on our cattle. So guns are a necessity there. No non-military citizen should have automatic weapons. I believe in the right to bear arms for protecting livestock and for food-hunting, sound ecological thinning of deer/bear populations and I do believe policemen need guns to fight crime."

When it comes to automatic guns, the area in which one lives helps shape opinions.

Thelma from Great Falls, MT, noted that "Guns are a big sport during hunting season here. My sons and grandson own guns. If people are responsible they should own guns. We depended on our father and brothers to hunt for food as we grew up."

Linda from Indianapolis, IN, said, "There should be gun control for irresponsible people, such as youth and people who are mentally challenged. My residence does not influence this response; I don't think there is any sacred place in the country that has not been affected by gun violence."

Tricia of Nashville, TN, explained her feelings are mixed regarding gun control. "I believe there are too many guns, but that perhaps it is too late to restrict them in a way that decreases crime without limiting freedoms or making gun ownership illegal entirely. And yes, my response is influenced by my family and where I live."

Krystal from Dickinson, ND, cautions, "I have always been around guns. You have to respect them."

Bri of North Carolina related an interesting story about her southern friends. "I was having lunch with a group of women and mentioned that someone asked me to be a replacement on a shooting team. They all reached for their handbags and pulled out guns for me to borrow! That pretty much says everything there is to say about this region of the country."

"We are gun people," proclaims Barbara of Nazareth, PA. "We are trap shooters and hunters and we favor it for our recreation."

Rachel from Downing, MO, was adamant. "Our country was founded on the right to bear arms and too much gun control will only leave guns in the hands of criminals. Additionally, guns are a way of life for some people to hunt for food which may restrict people from doing this."

Jeanine from Honolulu, HI, said her stance was really in support of gun control. "Obama is nuts; I joined the NRA as a lifetime member because I don't want my rights taken away. I don't own a gun. That's none of his business. The way he played with the US Constitution, I'm sure more things could have been subject to control. Big brother is watching!"

Amanda from Shamokin, PA, proclaims, "I am high on guns. My husband and I are hunters."

Not all the women were pro-guns. Some of them lived near a fatal shooting, the Sandy Hook Elementary School shooting, which occurred on December 14, 2012, in Newtown, Connecticut, when 20-year-old Adam Lanza fatally shot 20 children.

Gloria, who maintains two residences in Vermont and Connecticut notes, "I live 20 miles from Sandy Hook. I am so against assault weapons."

Having lived in the area near the Connecticut school shooting, Lisa from Stratford, CT, said, "Gun control is not needed. I don't own a gun, but I'm afraid of them. We need better background and mental evaluations."

Rachel from Peaks Island, ME, was beyond regular gun control. "If anything I believe in STRONGER gun control!!!"

North Dakota may be in gun/hunting country, but not all of its residents are pleased.

Frances of Fargo was influenced on one of her rotation rounds in medical school. "My first patient was a one-year old boy shot in the stomach with a gun. He would have stomach problems the rest of his life. This has stayed with me for years."

"Guns belong in a war," states Lisa of Indianapolis, IN. "I don't believe they belong anywhere else. Rifles or normal handguns I may support. My area doesn't influence my feelings about guns."

"No one should be allowed to buy an assault weapon," said Tania from Annapolis, MD.

Other women were more noncommittal.

"To each his own as long as it's done safely and responsibly," said Linda, Claremont, FL.

Tricia of Nashville, TN is more unsettled about guns. "I have mixed feelings. There are too many guns but that perhaps it is too late to restrict them in a way that decreases crime without limiting freedom or making gun ownership illegal entirely. I guess I'm influenced by my family and hometown."

According to Stephanie of Hill, UT, "There is nothing wrong with guns. I have guns. There is nothing else to do out here but shoot. They also are protection for many people."

Elizabeth of Beckley, WV, doesn't own a gun, but, "I support citizens' right to bear arms."

"I do not agree with banning guns," said Caroline from North Carolina. "Criminals will still find ways of obtaining guns illegally as they already do and the innocent will have no way of protecting themselves."

Joan of Califon, NJ, said, "I am pro gun. Every farmhouse in the country has a shotgun. As there is less crime in areas/cities that allow citizens to be armed and the criminals do not know who has a gun."

Courtney of Downing, MO, grew up hunting. Soon to graduate and go into accounting she explained, "That's all I know. The whole family, uncles, dad, everybody goes hunting especially during deer hunting season in November. Not to allow us to do that because we have guns would be ridiculous and insensitive."

Spring of Walls, MS, noted, "I was raised with a BB gun and learned how to use it. You should be allowed the choice."

Most of the women, regardless of their support or anti-gun sentiment all drew the line when it comes to easy access to machine guns or assault weapons.

As an example, Joyce Wirtz, VA, said, "Here in the south, guns are more prominent for hunting. But I'm not for machine guns."

Saralynn of Dakota City, MT, explained, "We are from Montana and guns are a big sport during hunting season. My sons and grandson own guns. If people are responsible they should own guns. We depend on our father and brothers to hunt for food as we grew up."

Though Janet of Winston-Salem, NC, doesn't own a gun, "I don't like government restrictions."

"In the wild west of New Mexico," says Mary of Albuquerque, "We have many people who have guns. I don't agree with it, but it's a way of life for the southwest."

Rheba of West Plains, MO, said, "I'm against gun control. It's why we have the Second Amendment. I don't have one but I want the right to."

"It's a personal choice," according to Cheryl of Rosemont, MN. "You should be able to own a gun in your own home as an insurance to protect yourself."

Lyneta of Spring Hill, TN, notes, "My birthplace, Wyoming, probably influences my opinion on gun control the most. I believe that some gun control is necessary, but never so much as to infringe on the 2nd amendment. (Laws restricting convicts, especially violent criminals, are good, for example.)"

Diane of Anchorage, AK, and her family own guns. "My husband and son share memories at the NRA, but I'm not opposed to some restrictions such as universal background checks, background checks at gun shows and for private sales."

"This country needs much stricter gun laws!" according to Jasmine of Dartmouth, MA.

"They are far too lax, it's absurd. I do not understand the resistance to background checks or limiting type and number of firearms allowed. Yes, I believe residents of my state agree."

Life at This Stage

"There is a fountain of youth: it is your mind, your talents, the creativity you bring to your life and the lives of people you love. When you learn to tap this source, you will truly have defeated age."

~ Sophia Loren

Most women were content with their lives at the present time. Women were asked to describe their attitude as either great/very good; okay, needs improvement, poor/very anxious, or no response. The majority were content. Of the responders, 48.1 percent rated their lives at the present as "good or great"; 36 percent as "okay"; 7.5 " acknowledge they are working on improving it; 5.6 percent rated it as "poor"; and 2.5 percent chose not to comment.

"I'm having a great time! I need to limit myself more in things I take on to accomplish so that I don't get tired. But I like doing them," according to Rheba of Cincinnati, OH.

"I love where I am at life and the age I am," said Judy of Indian Land, SC. "I am healthy enough to enjoy the community I live in and still have a little time to get the satisfaction of working as a private duty nurse in my community. I feel like I have won the jackpot of life. I feel very blessed. I LOVE the weather here in the south. I NEVER want to go up north again. I am glad to be a senior at this time. I feel very socially and physically and spiritually fulfilled and that says it all."

"My life is overflowing!" exclaims Frances of Fargo, ND. "Everything is so good; I have three wonderful kids and am really happy and madly in love."

For Tricia of Nashville, "Life now is exciting, difficult and fulfilling all at the same time!"

Stephanie of Hill, UT, says, "I am happy. I couldn't ask for more. I have a wonderful husband and a polite little boy. I am happy to be alive."

"Life is good!" according to Elaine of Ashville, AL. "I have time to write a little more, to play with my animals and my grandsons (not necessarily in that order). I also have time to give something back to society – I serve on the boards of my county library system and a charity organization. I have a comfortable income without having to work. A big positive is that I'm not nearly concerned with what people think about me as I used to."

Jill of Quincy, IL was enthusiastic in her response. "I am loving this age. It just seems to be getting better and better. My kids are 7 and 9 and so much fun! I have a wonderful husband, a good job and a lovely home. I only wonder how long I will feel this happy!"

Saralynn of Dakota City, NE, attributes her marital status as a prime key in her happiness at present. "We are still in the honeymoon phase so it's all great."

Kingstown, RI, resident Diane said, "I am very happy. I enjoy my career, my family and hope to live a long and healthy life. Every day is a new adventure. Whether it is a great day or a day I want to forget – I enjoy experiencing every emotion, interacting with friends, co-workers and family. To be honest – my life is terrific!"

"Life is a gift," said Tania of Annapolis, MD, "I feel so lucky."

Anka of Avon, IN, is also positive about this stage of her life. "I am happy, but my life is not at all what I imagined it even as recent as two years ago. God has a plan for me. I've accepted my failures and successes and I'm making ME happy… For once in my life!"

"I'm always happy," said Christy of Edmond, OK. "Looking back I would do some things differently, manage my free time better and pay little attention to things that do not matter."

Joyce of Wirtz, VA, is a tad less enthusiastic about life at this time. "Forget about the golden years. As long as I can get around things are good. I can volunteer or choose not to and not have to go to work."

According to Neva of Seattle, WA, "God has been so very good to me. Financially we do okay."

Some women cited their faith comes from their religious beliefs.

Spring from Wall, MS, explained, "My religion keeps me on top."

"At this stage in my life I am waiting to retire and move from Colorado back east," explained Pat from Arvedo.

Janet from Winston Salem, NC, said life is okay at this time for her. "Sometimes I'm not happy with personal life but I work at it. I have options and don't feel trapped if I need to make changes. I have the ability to support myself if needed as all women SHOULD."

Krystal from Dickinson, ND, a divorced mother of one child is a hotel front desk supervisor with no health insurance and several health issues she does not feel so positive about. "At this stage I am worried about my future."

Kathryn of Randolph, NJ, said, "Life is never without challenges, yet filled with love, blessings, plans and activities."

For Christy from Oklahoma, "I'm overall happy. Looking back – I would definitely do some things differently – manage my free time better and pay little attention to things that do not matter."

At 55, Brie of Clayton, NC, says, "I like where I am right now. I didn't know what 55 would be like. Now that it's here, I'm doing well."

Phyllis of Fountain Valley, CA, said, "I am happy with my life. Happier than I have ever been."

Some women were passive about their status.

Lisa of Stratford, CT, said, "It could definitely be better, but you have to go with what you have"

Vicky of Deleware said, "I'm not overjoyed with the state of the world and health issues, but basically, okay."

Dianne whose home is in Alaska was on the same page. "Mostly positive but I do have great frustration with the Republican Congress and its failure to act in the best interests of the country."

Lisa of Indianapolis, IN, qualified her answer. "I feel this stage of my life is okay, if I look at it from a philosophical level. I am thankful for what I have. Beyond this, though, I feel I would have been at a different place at this point and more soulfully fulfilled and confident with real and wise experiences under my belt."

Some women expressed they had not yet arrived at their desired place in their lives. "I'm not there yet," Alyssia of San Pedro, CA noted. "I feel that I'm mature enough to reach my goals and am almost there. I'm on the road to where I want to be."

Jeanine of Honolulu, HI, finds comfort in the resolution of some critical issues. "I feel like things are getting better in the sense that a lot of issues like death, and having trust are starting to be resolved. Almost to a point that my own life the way I want it to be."

Brie of Columbia, MD, said, "My life is not too shabby, but could improve."

Joan of Brockton, MA, said, "I could be doing better; maybe next year."

Though happy at present it's not the end all and be all for Linda of IN. "I feel pretty satisfied, I'm still alive and living and you cannot ask for more than that."

"I'm satisfied and excited for the future," claims Marie of Bowling Green, KY. "But I'm not content because I don't have everything I want out of life."

Many of those women who expressed their disappointment in not attaining their goals were still working at accomplishing their goals. "I feel I need to work harder at my schooling and work on my time management," said Deda of Jersey City, NJ.

There were a few who were very negative in their responses. Personal relationships or the lack of them was one element cited by women. Financial stress was still another issue.

"I am stagnant and confused," said Belinda of Portage, IN.

Mary of Monsey, NY, expressed her desperation. "My life has been a failure. I am broke living in a boarding house with no job and alone."

Barbra of Irvington, NJ, said, "I just live day to day. I expect nothing from anyone. I just want to get by. The whole journey has been a train wreck."

"I am very worried about my future," said Krystal of North Dakota.

"In some ways I'm scared," said Cristina of Washington, NJ. "But in other ways I realize my strength to persevere."

"It's tough right now," said Caroline of South Carolina. "Sometimes I feel like I stretch myself thin. I find that I get stressed a lot. I know I am working towards a goal though as long as I keep moving forwards, I will be happy."

"It's bittersweet for me. I am not afraid of death because I have a strong faith that something wonderful is to come, but I will miss my life and loved ones," said Barbara of East Syracuse, NY.

Serious and threatening health issues were reasons some women did not view their lives at this stage as completely positive or worry free.

Anita of Great Falls, MT, said, "I am very worried because of my recent severe allergy to mercury, which is in all electronics and fluorescent lights. I live in a lot of pain now and am severely limited as to where I can go."

Barbara of Chester, NJ, also spoke in regards to her health. "Today, I'm great. Last week, not so good. I take one day at a time, answer to no one but myself."

"Right now, I'm making changes in my life to make it better," said Eileen of Las Vegas, NV.

For Lyneta of Spring Hill, TN, it is a good time. "I think I'm in the right place now. We've worked hard to get here and love being able to guide our adult children as well."

"Overall, I feel great about this stage of my life," said Jasmine of Dartmouth, MA. "I have a strong career, a Master's degree and a new home soon. Actively seeking a life partner and hoping to be a mother someday. There's been a lot of positive change in my life over the past few years and I am excited for the future."

Conclusions

This four-year study taught me a great deal. It changed my perceptions and also strengthened my belief in the power of women. What were the results of the survey? Are women more alike than different?

1. First the surprises. One of the biggest revelations was the majority of women said they were **not** in favor of the country approving Spanish as a second official language. English remains their choice. The consensus was that if their ancestors had to follow the rules for immigration to this country, then so should newcomers. This was not only the case for legal entrance to the country, but also the necessity to learn the English language. There is a "my parents/grandparents/great grandparents, families had to learn it, and so should anyone else entering the country" mentality.

Women cited the ample opportunities for immigrants to take ESL classes as a pathway to assimilation in their new chosen country. Other women pointed to other countries where immigrants must learn their accepted language. Their reaction? It should be the same in America.

2. It became apparent that women have shifted their attitudes toward practicing religion. In lieu of the observation of more traditional values/practices and tenets of a specific church or house of worship, there is a tendency to cite their "spiritual" connection. This was true even for women who had strong affiliations with an established church. Religion/spirituality has become a personal matter.

3. I was pleased to notice that the majority of the women took pride in education, and some made it quite clear that they learned from their parents that upward mobility was only attained through a college education or advanced technological learning. Others viewed the teaching of the value of money as a key component of every child's education for an ultimate stable economy. On this point, several said they do not rely on credit cards in any way.

4. I was thrilled with the reaction of women who strongly connected to their roots. This is true whether they were born here or elsewhere. Our United States is comprised of 50 states, each different and wonderful in their own ways. From weather to foods to politics, the respondents took pride in their regional heritage.

Even with blocks of areas by which several states are defined as New England or the Deep South, women are very much aware of the districts in which they live and celebrate those traditions, foods and culture with enthusiasm and spirit often calling themselves "proud." They acknowledge their traits, their dialects, their political leanings, the economic realities of living there, the opportunities or lack thereof for cultural events and many more aspects of their daily lives.

5. Women no longer go to work and watch TV all night. I was elated at the variety of hobbies and sports the women actively took part in contributing to their wellbeing. There were hobbies I wasn't familiar with, but all the women celebrated their unique pastimes.

6. With all the talk of divorce, I was amazed at the large number of women who are married. Several spoke of ways to maintain their relationships; others, more or less, said they learned to live with whatever flaws or negativities exist within their relationships. Those women who were divorced or single parents, seemed to be negotiating their lives well, though admitting it "wasn't easy."

7. While women were upfront about their dislikes of certain politicians and policies, none rose to a level of hatred or total blind support of their states and the red, white, and blue. Many put the blame of inaction on certain policies on the inhouse fighting between the two major parties.

These women had the pulse of the country and were hoping and pushing for the best for each other.

8. As I anticipated, many respondents indicated valid concerns for present and future health care. Several had good suggestions regarding the funding of facilities for the elderly. A vast majority acknowledged the need to financially plan for their retirement years when health issues may arise.

The disappointments.
As a writer and avid reader, I was disappointed about the lower number of "avid readers." I attribute the figures as an indication of the lack of time caring for children, working outside the home, interests, care giving, etc., which leaves but a small chunk of time for reading. As we women juggle our multi-level tasks and lives, I am impressed with the fact that we are indeed women who dwell in possibilities!

You can see where you stand by taking the following survey.

Questionnaire

PLEASE PRINT ALL ANSWERS: *Only first names and last initials will be used.* *

NAME: _____

City: State: _____

Age Group: Circle one:

    (20-30)   (60-70)
    (30-40)   (70-80)
    (40 50)   (80-90)
    (50-60)   (90-100)

Highest level of Education:

    Elementary school   tech school
    H.S.   college graduate
    College   graduate degree
    attended business   MD or PHD:

Career: Title/description Length in this career: _____

_____

Why did you choose this career? _____
_____

Advantages? _____

Drawbacks? _____

What is the public's most common misperception about your career?
_____
_____

Have you had more than one career? If so, what was it? Why did you change? _____
_____

How would you counsel a young girl/woman considering going into this career?_____
_____

Is there a discrepancy between what you earn and a male counterpart earns on your job? _____
_____

Marital Status: Single / married/ Separated / Divorced/ Widowed (circle one)

How long? _____

On a scale of 1 (poor) to 10 (great) how satisfying is/was your relationship? _____

How would you change your relationship if you could? _____
_____

How many children do you have? _____

How old were you when you had your first child? _____

Should all women have children? Why? Why not? Opinion about single parenting. _____
_____

Should all gender couples have/adopt children? Why? Why not? _____
_____

How important is religion in your life? To what degree are you involved in religious activities/charities/committees/fundraising; instruction/camps; choral groups? _____
_____

Do you see a breakdown in morality in present day America? To what do you attribute that? _____
_____

What is your feeling of comfort regarding the state of the US economy? Why? _____
_____

Do you feel that your family is better off economically/ the same/ or worse today than when you were a child? _____
_____

On a scale of 1 (the least concern) to 10 how concerned are you about your health and health care options in the future? What are your specific concerns? _____
_____

What is your greatest concern about aging yourself and, if applicable, aging parents/grandparents? _____
_____

Solutions? _____
_____

Have you ever served in the military? Length of service. Branch? Rank?
_____
_____

What are your feelings about sending your son/daughter off to war?
_____
_____

Residence: Circle one: Do you own a home; rent a home; rent an apartment/ own a condo/townhouse; live with parents or relatives

Hobbies/recreation? _____
_____

Do you feel that you and your partner are socially active or have other commitments – work/ children/ health/aging parents/ tight finances put a crimp on your fun time? _____
_____

Are you a (Circle one): Frequent traveler; occasional traveler; rarely travel; never travel?

Have you ever lived in another country outside USA? Where? Why? How long? _____
_____

What US city would you most like to visit? Why? _____
_____

What would be your ideal vacation? _____
_____

Circle one: Are you an avid reader? Occasional reader? Never read books.

Do you belong to a book club and if so, what have you gained from being a member? _____
_____

Do you prefer small town rural life/ suburbs/big city action (Circle one)

Circle one: How often does your family eat out a week? Once/ Twice/ Three or more times/ rarely; never.

What is your family's favorite meal that you prepare? _____
_____

When it comes to food shopping circle all that apply: I take advantage of supermarket chain store sales; I shop only at savings stores like BJ's Wholesale Club; Sam's Club; Costco Wholesale; Wal-Mart etc.; I buy only brand names regardless of the cost savings; I am an extreme couponer.

How important is television viewing in your home? Are you content with your answer? _____
_____

Do you have a pet? What kind? What has your pet brought to you/your/ family's life? _____
_____

How has the area of the country in which you live (east; north; south; west) influenced your lifestyle and your way of thinking? Why do you think this is so? _____
_____

What is your biggest fear? Disappointments? _____
_____

What is your fondest dream? _____
_____

How soon do you anticipate that dream being fulfilled? _____

In what ways have your parents influenced your lifestyle choices?

Are you a sport fans? Which sports/teams? _____

Circle which you enjoy and the frequency you partake: Concerts; theater; movies; museums: once a year; twice a year; three times or more: rarely; never.

Should the USA officially become a bi-lingual country? If so, which should be the second language spoken? Why? Why not? _____

How prepared are you/spouse/partner for retirement? (Do not divulge any financial details.) _____

How prepared are you/spouse/partner for your final expenses? (Preparing a will; designating guardians; choosing a final resting site.)

What is your opinion on gun control? Does your residence in a particular section of the country influence your decision? _____

In general, how do you feel about your life at this stage of time?

Sources

National Review
Dennis Prage 4/7/15

Gallup's Annual Values and Beliefs Poll, 6/20.15

The National Opinion Research Center at the University of Chicago, 2014

Bureau of Labor and Statistics

Pew Forum on Religion and Public Life

Ticketmaster's 2014 Live Event Attendance Study

National Endowment for the Arts, 2012 book reading survey
Rasmussen poll, 2014 indicated that 83 percent of those participating say that English should be the official language of the United States
The typical American spends four hours and 51 minutes in front of a TV screen per day according to a report from ratings company, Nielson

Star Ledger, "Divided We Stand," April 28, 2014

May 2011 Harris Poll on pet ownership

March 2016 Harris Poll conducted for Nationwide Retirement Institute

Glamour magazine Chase study 2016

American Pet Products Association (APPA), total pet industry expenditures reached $60.59 billion in 2015. That's up from $58.04 billion in 2014.

Acknowledgments

Gaining the attention of women across the country was not an easy project as I mentioned earlier. I owe a great deal of gratitude to the following individuals who were able to connect me with friends and relatives throughout this country.

Bea Hailes, a fellow book club member and friend who was helpful in locating women from all over the country to help with the survey.

Roberta Hoffman, one of my co-"Zombie chick" dancer friends who extended herself to find other women in the south to help make the book possible.

David Holton, who similarly used his contacts out in the west to garner some wonderful women to put their stamp on this project.

The Roger Williams Zoo, RI.

And a resounding thank you to all the women who participated in this important project. As the title of the book implies: We all DO dwell in possibilities!

Other Books by Carlotta G. Holton

Non fiction
Getting Out of Limbo

Fiction
Salem Pact
Touching the Dead
Vampire Resurrection
Deadly Innocence
Grave Matters